Language in
Education

ALSO AVAILABLE FROM BLOOMSBURY

Language, Education and Discourse, edited by Joseph Foley

Language and Education, by M. A. K Halliday (edited by Jonathan J. Webster)

Advances in Language and Education, edited by Anne McCabe,
Mick O'Donnell and Rachel Whittaker

Social Identities and Multiple Selves in Foreign Language Education,
edited by Damian J. Rivers and Stephanie Ann Houghton

*Language Learning in New English Contexts: Studies in
Acquisition and Development*, edited by Rita Elaine Silver,
Christine C. M. Goh and Lubna Alsagoff

Developing Materials for Language Teaching, by Brian Tomlinson

A Companion Website is available at
www.bloomsbury.com/language-in-education-9781441151810

Language in Education

Social Implications

Edited by
RITA ELAINE SILVER
AND
SOE MARLAR LWIN

BLOOMSBURY
LONDON · NEW DELHI · NEW YORK · SYDNEY

Bloomsbury Academic
An imprint of Bloomsbury Publishing Plc

50 Bedford Square	1385 Broadway
London	New York
WC1B 3DP	NY 10018
UK	USA

www.bloomsbury.com

First published 2014

British Library Cataloguing-in-Publication Data
A catalogue record for this book is available from the British Library.

ISBN: HB: 978-1-4411-5194-0
PB: 978-1-4411-5181-0
ePub: 978-1-4411-5077-6
ePDF: 978-1-4411-9412-1

Library of Congress Cataloging-in-Publication Data
Language in education : social implications / Edited by Rita Elaine Silver and
Soe Marlar Lwin.
pages cm. – (Bloomsbury Advances in Semiotics)
Includes bibliographical references and index.
ISBN 978-1-4411-5194-0 (hardcover : alk. paper) – ISBN 978-1-4411-5181-0 (pbk. : alk.
paper) – ISBN 978-1-4411-5077-6 (ebook (epub) – ISBN 978-1-4411-9412-1 (ebook (pdf)
1. Language and education. 2. Language and languages–Study and teaching.
3. Language policy. 4. Interdisciplinary approach to education. 5. Education–Social
aspects. 6. Sociolinguistics. I. Silver, Rita, editor of compilation. II. Lwin,
Soe Marlar, editor of compilation.
P40.8.L3675 2013
306.44–dc23
2013018706

Typeset by Newgen Knowledge Works (P) Ltd., Chennai, India
Printed and bound in Great Britain

Contents

List of Contributors

Lubna Alsagoff has a PhD in Linguistics from Stanford University (USA). She is currently an Associate Professor and holds an appointment as Associate Dean, Office of Education Research, at the National Institute of Education (NIE), Nanyang Technological University (NTU) (Singapore). Her research examines the ways in which Englishes vary in different sociocultural contexts. She is co-editor (with Sandra McKay, Guangwei Hu and Willy Renandya) of *Principles and Practices for Teaching English as an International Language* (2012) and *The Global-Local Interface, Language Choice and Hybridity* (forthcoming) (with Rani Rubdy), and author of *A Visual Grammar of English* (2009), as well as numerous journal articles and book chapters on these topics.

Rukmini Becerra Lubies is a PhD student at the University of Washington (USA). Her focus is language, literacy and culture, and her broad research interest is bilingual and intercultural education for indigenous and non-indigenous groups in South America. Originally from Chile, she has earned a professional degree as a language teacher and a master degree in Linguistics, both from University of Chile.

Paul Grahame Doyle is the Programme Director (Effective Communication) of the English Language Institute of Singapore. He obtained his PhD in Linguistics from Lancaster University (UK), and is an experienced language teacher and teacher educator, having worked in Scotland, Sudan, India, Indonesia and Singapore on developing language and communication skills for a range of learners. His current research interests include examining how language used by teachers and students across the school curriculum can influence the development of disciplinary thinking and literacies, and the use of corpus-based methods to deepen understanding of disciplinary variation in classroom discourse.

Christine C. M. Goh has a PhD in Linguistics from Lancaster University (UK) and is Professor of linguistics and language education at the NIE, NTU (Singapore). She is interested in oracy development among English language learners and its relationship with language and literacy development. She has taught English teaching methodology courses to pre-service and in-service teachers, as well as academic courses on linguistics, language acquisition and oracy research to undergraduate and graduate students. She has also published many refereed articles and books in the areas mentioned.

Theres Grüter has a PhD in Linguistics from McGill University (Canada). She is currently an Assistant Professor in the Department of Second Language Studies at the University of Hawai'i at Mānoa (USA). Her research investigates how various learner types – typically and atypically developing, monolingual and bilingual children, as well as child and adult second language learners – acquire and process language. She is particularly interested in how factors beyond the grammar proper, such as working memory, language experience and understanding of discourse, contribute to the development of grammatical abilities.

Anthea Fraser Gupta (PhD) is a sociolinguist with a special interest in English as a world language and in first language acquisition in a bilingual context. She has had posts at the National University of Singapore and the University of Leeds (UK), and is now retired from full-time work. Her most recent publications are on issues in Standard English and on grammatical variation in English. She lives in Australia.

Ho Chee Lick obtained his PhD in Linguistics from Kansas University (USA) in 1989. He has been teaching at the National University of Singapore since 1990, in the fields of general linguistics, sociolinguistics and cross-cultural communication and translation. He is also a passionate musician and painter.

Francis M. Hult is an Associate Professor at the Centre for Languages and Literature, Lund University (Sweden). He holds a PhD in Educational Linguistics from the University of Pennsylvania Graduate School of Education (USA). Hult's research work uses discourse analytic approaches to investigate issues of societal multilingualism and language policy, with particular attention to education. His books include the *Handbook of Educational Linguistics* (2008, Wiley-Blackwell, with Bernard Spolsky), *Directions and Prospects for Educational Linguistics* (2010, Springer) and *Educational Linguistics in Practice* (2011, Multilingual Matters, with Kendall King). He is a member of the advisory committee for the international Language Policy Research Network (LPREN).

Galyna Kogut is a Research Associate in English Language and Literature at the NIE, NTU (Singapore) where she is pursuing her PhD. She has worked on a series of research projects focusing on classroom interactions, collaborative learning and reading comprehension. Her research interests include collaborative learning, dialogic teaching and classroom discourse. Prior to joining the NIE, Galyna worked as a teacher of English as a Second Language for five years in Ukraine and in Singapore.

Soe Marlar Lwin has a PhD in Language Studies from the National University of Singapore. She is currently an Assistant Professor at the NIE, NTU (Singapore) and teaches courses on introduction to the study of language, analysing language use and oracy development in the BA and MA (Applied Linguistics) programmes. Her research interests include studies of narrative structures, multimodal analysis of oral storytelling discourse and the use of narrative in language and literacy education. She is the author of articles on these topics and of *Narrative Structures in Burmese Folk Tales* (2010).

Raslinda A. R. has a Master of Education from the NIE, NTU (Singapore) where she is currently pursuing her PhD in Applied Linguistics. She is working concurrently as a Teaching Fellow at Office of Education Research, NIE. She works closely with teachers and in teacher development as part of her involvement in ongoing research projects. Her research interests are in language acquisition, language assessment and classroom discourse with a focus on student peer interactions. She was a teacher and Head of Department/English Language in a Singapore government primary school before joining the NIE.

Rita Elaine Silver has a PhD in Educational Linguistics from the Graduate School of Education at the University of Pennsylvania (USA). She is currently an Associate Professor in English Language and Literature at the NIE, NTU (Singapore). She was a teacher of English as a Second/Foreign Language in Japan and the USA for 14 years before turning her attention to language teacher education. Currently, she teaches courses in language development, language teaching methods and literacy instruction, primarily for teachers at the primary grade levels. Her research focuses on teacher-student classroom interactions. She is co-editor, with Christine C. M. Goh and Lubna Alsagoff, of *Language Learning in New English Contexts: Studies of Acquisition and Development* (2009) and with Wendy Bokhorst-Heng of *Quadrilingual Education in Singapore: Pedagogical Innovation in Language Education* (2014).

Peter Teo obtained his PhD in Linguistics from Lancaster University (UK). He is currently an Associate Professor at the NIE, NTU (Singapore) where his teaching and research interests converge in the areas of Critical Discourse Analysis, critical literacy and writing pedagogy. He is a teacher educator at heart and hopes to inspire his students to embrace a critical attitude towards language and teaching.

Manka M. Varghese has a PhD in Educational Linguistics from the Graduate School of Education at the University of Pennsylvania (USA). She is currently an Associate Professor in Language, Literacy and Culture at the University of Washington's College of Education in Seattle, Washington (USA). Her scholarship and teaching focus on three areas of immigration and schooling: language minority teacher education and professional identities; transitions to higher education for language minority students; the intersections of race, immigration and language teaching in the USA and internationally. She has published numerous books and journal articles on these topics.

1

What Is the Role of Language in Education?

Soe Marlar Lwin and Rita Elaine Silver

INTRODUCTION

Language is pervasive in our lives, with many roles and purposes. In almost every moment of our waking lives, and often even in our dreams, we make use of language. It is a tool for many purposes – exchanging information, expressing desires and emotions, recording or organizing our thoughts, to name just a few. Among all the roles that language plays, this volume is particularly interested in understanding the role of language in education.

In this chapter, we give you some background for reading this book. We look at some of the connections between language and education that we think are important. We also introduce the purpose and organization of the book as a whole. First, we provide some preliminary comments on a few fundamental properties of language that we think will be useful to you.

THE NATURE OF LANGUAGE

A discussion of the role of language in education might begin with the question *What is language?* People usually think of words (or vocabulary) and grammar when they think of language. It seems that words are most easily recognized as an important or fundamental unit to make meaning. However, words are, in fact, made up of smaller elements such as sounds and **morphemes**. Think about the difference between *book* and *hook* or *woman* and *women* – a change in a single sound also changes the meaning. Thus, although words and grammar are often described as the nuts and bolts of language, they represent only two among many aspects. Besides words and grammar, other aspects of language include sounds, meanings and use.

Moreover, knowing a language entails more than knowing the meaning of a word, the grammatical rules and the sounds. In an article for early childhood teachers, Timothy Jay (2007) cites an example of one child calling another a *poop-head*. On one level, the word was 'correct' in the sense that it conveyed the meaning the child wanted to convey. On another level, it is unlikely that an adult would choose this particular term to convey displeasure with another person because the adult would have learned a set of rules for appropriate use as well as rules for vocabulary, grammar and sounds. From this sort of example, we can see that knowing a language means more than knowing how to use vocabulary and grammar. It also means knowing the rules for appropriate use in a variety of social situations.

It might be more helpful to describe language in terms of how it works, for example in terms of physical, cognitive and social aspects. From the physical aspect, language can be described as a motor skill which involves the use of certain physiological features that humans possess, such as the tongue, lips, vocal cords and other speech organs which are suitable for articulating sounds used in speech. In its cognitive aspect, language involves a speaker's knowledge and processing of sounds, morphemes, words and rules of grammar. The social aspect of language, on the other hand, underlines the use of language for interaction with people and explains language as a social phenomenon. From this perspective, differences among languages or within a language are related to various social factors such as different situations or purposes of using the language and different identities of participants in an interaction.

Given these various aspects of language, it is tempting to describe language simply as a system of communication which we use to convey information. This is the sort of definition found in the *Oxford Dictionary Online*. However this leads to more questions, such as *How is human language different from the communication systems used by other species?* and *Is language unique to human beings?* It is evident that other species do communicate with members of their own species, and in some cases even with other species, using certain kind of communicative signals (e.g. Birds sing. Dogs bark.). It is, therefore, important to recognize some of the features which make human language unique.

Many people have been interested in investigating the differences and similarities between human language and communication systems of other species. An essay titled *The Origin of Speech* by Charles F. Hockett (1960) is often claimed to be the earliest investigation of this topic. Hockett outlined 13 characteristics which he explained as the 'design-features' that separate human language from animal communication systems. However, since Hockett's study, others have discovered more about the communicative abilities of various animals and these more recent studies have proved that many of the features proposed by Hockett as characteristics of human language are also present to some extent in certain animal communication systems.

Nevertheless, there remain a few features which have yet to be found, or which are very limited, in the communication systems of other species. Features which are highlighted as unique characteristics or essential properties of human language include 'duality of patterning', 'productivity', 'displacement', 'arbitrariness' and 'cultural transmission'. Understanding these five features can also help you to better understand fundamental issues in language learning, language use and the social implications of language in educational settings.

Duality of patterning

In the most fundamental sense of speech production, speakers of a language arrange individual sounds (e.g. /p/, /t/, /ɪ/) – meaningless elements on their own – into meaningful units (e.g. *pit* or *tip*). Notice that the order of individual sounds can be rearranged to produce different words with different meanings. This feature of combining meaningless individual sounds in different ways to produce meaningful units (words or utterances) is called 'duality of patterning' (or simply 'duality'). Duality is recognized as a feature which distinguishes human language from the communication systems of other species because, unlike human language, a **communicative signal** in animal communication cannot be broken down into smaller elements. For example, a cat's *meow* cannot be broken down into *m + e + o + w* which can then be manipulated or rearranged in another way (e.g. *woem*) to get a different meaningful unit. In essence, the feature of duality captures the idea that a human language has individual sounds at one level and distinct meanings resulting from arrangements and rearrangements of these sounds at another level. Duality is useful for understanding how language is built in layers: Distinct sounds, as the smallest elements, can be organized into meaningful units like words which can in turn be organized into bigger and more complex meaningful units like phrases and clauses. When we understand duality, we can also understand why it is important to study the structure of language at various levels (i.e. sounds, words, phrases, clauses, sentences and texts).

Productivity

Closely related to duality is the feature of 'productivity', which is sometimes referred to as 'creativity' or 'open-endedness'. The fact that human language is made up of small distinct elements which can be organized in more than one way to get bigger and more complex units suggests that the creation of new words, utterances or sentences is infinite. Even though a particular language makes use of only a fixed set of sounds, it has the capacity to create new words by manipulating these distinct sounds and to convey an infinite number of messages by constructing a vast number and range of utterances or sentences. Productivity is recognized as a feature which makes human language unique because the signals in communication systems of other species are not only limited in number (e.g. only 4 signals for cicadas and 36 vocal calls for vervet monkeys), but also fixed to specific objects or occasions and cannot be manipulated to express a new meaning. Experiments done on the vervet monkey have shown that although they have specific signals for *snake* and *eagle*, they failed to produce a new signal when they saw a creature that looked like a flying snake. Productivity as a design feature of human language is useful for understanding how it is possible for speakers of a language to express limitless meanings, creating new or novel **linguistic forms** as need arises. Words and expressions which have been created to talk about new inventions or developments in science and information technology (e.g. *chloroform, petrology, SMS, blog*, etc.) are good examples of the productive nature of human language. Understanding the linguistic creativity of human language is helpful for an exploration of how speakers of a language can adapt existing linguistic forms in possibly infinite ways to suit a range of situations and purposes, and how new linguistic forms can be created to express new or novel meanings when there is a need.

Displacement

Another fundamental property of human language is the feature of 'displacement'. Language enables us to talk about things, people and events which are not present in our immediate environment. For example, we can talk about our last vacation, write greetings and wishes for a friend's coming birthday even though these events, places and people are not immediately present. Animal communication, on the other hand, is in general designed to refer rather exclusively to the objects in the immediate environment or the events happening in the present moment. For example, a cat would not be able to communicate about the meal it had yesterday or a meal that it would like to have next week by meowing. Although studies of the communication system of bees have shown how bees can communicate about a food source that is removed in space, further experiments have proved their displacement ability to be very limited (e.g. only for the most recent food source and only in terms of horizontal distance). Recognizing displacement as a design feature of human language is helpful for recognizing why the development of **decontextualized language** (i.e. the ability to use language to talk about what is beyond 'here and now') is considered important in child language acquisition and learning (Snow et al., 1995). As a child develops cognitively and socially, the child needs to use language to communicate about things, people and events which are not present in the immediate environment. Moreover, since most school tasks require children to talk or write about things, people and events which are not present, happening at that moment, or with background knowledge not shared by all, the ability to use decontextualize language is crucial for academic learning. Therefore, it is useful to understand displacement as not only a property of human language which distinguishes it from animal communication, but also a feature of language development.

Arbitrariness

The capacity to refer to things, people and events which are not in the immediate environment of the speaker (i.e. displacement) and to generate new linguistic forms (i.e. productivity) is possible because of another property of human language called 'arbitrariness'. In any human language, there is the absence of natural or inherent connection between a linguistic form (e.g. sounds, words, grammatical structure) and its meaning. For example, the word *red* in English does not have to be written in red ink to mean the particular colour it represents. In addition, the same colour is represented by a different word *merah* in Malay. There is no inherent connection between the idea and the sounds or word used to represent the idea. Therefore, we can say that in human language the relationship between a linguistic form and its meaning is arbitrary, allowing different forms in different languages. **Onomatopoeic words** (e.g. *bang, woof woof*) may seem to have natural connections between the form and meaning because these resemble the actual sounds made by objects or animals. However, notice that different languages have different linguistic forms to represent the sound made by the same type of animal (e.g. a dog's bark is represented as *woof woof* in English, but *kong kong* in Balinese and *wang wang* in Mandarin Chinese). This raises the question of whether such onomatopoeic words are truly iconic.

Unlike human language, each signal in an animal communication system is fixed, with a specific meaning to refer to a specific object or situation at a specific time (e.g. a particular type of call to warn of a particular type of danger). Therefore, the relationship between an animal's communicative signal and its meaning is said to be indexical: A causal or sequential relationship exists. Although it is evident that a similar indexical relationship exists between some linguistic forms and their meanings in human language (e.g. the word *Exit* above the door of a building), most linguistic forms in human language are arbitrary. The connection between a linguistic form and its meaning is decided collectively by speakers of that particular language, in other words, the connection is established through social conventions.

Why is it useful to be aware of arbitrariness as a property of human language and a fundamental aspect of language development and language use? Arbitrariness highlights the fact that there is more to knowing a language than knowing a collection of linguistic forms (i.e. sounds or symbols representing meaningful words). At the most basic level, the process of learning how to speak and listen involves the ability to manipulate and interpret sounds to make meanings with a communication system accepted by a community of users. Similarly, the process of learning how to read and write in a language involves, at the most basic level, an ability to interpret graphic symbols and use them to make meanings for a community of users.

Cultural transmission

In spite of all its complexity, most children acquire a language and seem to be able to use it without much conscious effort. What makes this possible? We are not born with the ability to speak a particular language (e.g. we are not born as speakers of Chinese or English or Spanish). We acquire a language by using the language in a particular culture and by interacting with other speakers in our daily lives. This process of acquiring a language which is passed on from an experienced user to a learner or one generation to the next was first explained by Hockett (1960) as 'tradition' or 'traditional transmission'. Others (e.g. Yule, 2010) have referred to this aspect of language as 'cultural transmission'. Human language is non-instinctive: We do not inherit a specific language in the same way we inherit genetic traits such as brown hair or blue eyes. We learn the language which is used with and around us. If a child of Chinese origin is brought up by English-speaking parents in an English-speaking culture, the child will grow up speaking English.

The feature of cultural transmission distinguishes human language from animal communication because, for the most part, signals are produced instinctively in animal communication. Although studies of bird songs have shown that certain species of birds learn to acquire varied versions of songs depending on the geographic area in which the bird inhabits, many aspects of it is still innate – the bird sings a 'simplified' version of the song even if it has never heard it sung. In general, an animal will use signals which are instinctive to its species to communicate regardless of the surroundings in which it is raised – a kitten that grows up among cows will still meow. For a human child with normal cognitive development and social environment to use language to interact with other speakers, the process of language acquisition may seem automatic. However, investigation into language development has produced strong evidence that language is non-instinctive and must be acquired by interacting with other speakers of the language.

Recognizing culture transmission as a feature of human language is important because first it helps us to understand that language acquisition is not only a cognitive process but also a social process (i.e. individual learners acquire a language by interacting with those around in socially and culturally relevant ways). Secondly, it highlights the importance of understanding the sociocultural factors leading to variations in a language spoken by different groups of people (e.g. variation based on growing up in different regions of the same country) and also the close connections between one's language and identity. In other words, acknowledging cultural transmission raises our awareness of why language differences reflect speakers' cultural and social backgrounds in spite of having some commonalities such as duality of patterning, productivity, displacement and arbitrariness.

In all of these features – duality, productivity, displacement, arbitrariness and cultural transmission – we see that human language has social implications for the creation of meanings.

LINGUISTIC INQUIRY

The study of language, or **linguistics** as it is commonly known, investigates universality as well as diversity of languages, giving rise to various sub-fields such as psycholinguistics, sociolinguistics, forensic linguistics, educational linguistics, etc. No matter the sub-field, all linguistic inquiry involves a systematic exploration of language data to find out what language is, how language is used, how language is learned and so on. **Linguistic inquiry** tries to find answers to questions about language in general, developing models or theories about sounds, structures and meanings as properties which all languages have in common. Linguistic inquiry also investigates the relationship between features of a particular language and the impact of variables such as the cultural practices of speakers, social background, functional factors, institutional structure, etc. Any of these ways of studying language can be helpful as they provide information on the nature of language as a cognitive and social phenomenon and for investigating the roles language plays in different settings.

Understanding linguistic inquiry is a crucial part of understanding how linguists think and how we investigate language – in educational settings and elsewhere. An essential part of linguistic inquiry, or any scientific inquiry, is observation. However, observation can be tricky because we might tend to notice what is unusual, rather than what is typical, and to understand language we must observe the typical as well as the atypical. For example, a 3-year-old American girl was in the car with her family driving through an agricultural area. The girl pointed out the window and said, *Look! A sprINK-ler system!* The whole family laughed because *sprinkler system* was an unusual vocabulary item for a child of that age and because she pronounced the sounds so distinctly. The family remembered this incident many years later because it was cute and funny – and atypical for a child of her age. Probably everyone has examples of these sorts of anecdotal observations because they are fun and interesting. However, these sorts of observation are not very useful for understanding what language is and how it is used. For understanding about language, we need systematic, rather than anecdotal, observation. Systematic observations allow us to discern patterns, so we can identify what is typical or unique. Research on language in education is made up of systematic observations done with tools including student tests, lesson observations, interviews and a variety of others.

This volume puts together findings based on systematic observations from various sub-fields of linguistics. The authors of each chapter summarize findings from some of the most important research and discuss how these findings can help you understand fundamental issues related to the role and social implications of language in education. We hope our discussions of these findings will provide an informed way of thinking about issues of language in education and enrich your perception of the connections between language and education.

LANGUAGE IN EDUCATIONAL SETTINGS

Language instruction

Just as language learning requires cultural transmission with cognitive and social processes coming into play, **language instruction** has cultural, cognitive and social aspects. In this book, we are particularly interested in the juxtaposition of language learning and use in educational settings. When thinking of language in education, you might think first of language and literacy instruction. This is usually – but not always – done in the dominant home language of the students. This can include basic reading and writing skills taught in the early years of schooling or literature studies in later years. These classes can also include more advanced literacy skills such as learning to do formal presentations, write research papers, use persuasive language in academic discussions, read and write analytically.

Alternatively, you might think of **foreign language learning** or **second language learning**. For example, many of us have spent years studying French, German, Spanish, Japanese, Chinese, etc. (with mixed success!) in the predominantly English-based curricula of American or British schools. Or, in a world in which English learning is increasingly a part of educational systems internationally, you might think of classes for English as a foreign language (EFL) or English as a second language (ESL). Traditionally, 'foreign language' refers to learning a language in environments in which that language is not commonly used outside the classroom (e.g. English in Dubai, Korea, Brazil). 'Second language' usually refers to learning a language in environments where it is common outside the classroom but it is not the language of the student's home (e.g. students going to Vietnam to study Vietnamese or to France to study French). There are also bilingual education systems which intentionally teach two (or more) languages along with other academic content (e.g. science, mathematics, history, film studies). In these courses, the goal is for students to learn the subject matter and the language simultaneously. These are all examples of formal language teaching contexts for students who do not use the instructed language as their dominant home language.

Medium of instruction

Language in education isn't only about learning to read and write or about formal language teaching. An important role that language plays in schools is as a **medium of instruction**. Mercer (2007) explains that the specific aims of formal education involve helping pupils acquire knowledge about particular subjects, such as science, mathematics, arts, etc. How does a teacher help a learner to do things and to acquire subject knowledge? Primarily through language! In school, students not only learn a language (English, French, Mandarin, etc.) as a curriculum subject, but also use language for learning other subjects. At all levels of education and for all subject matter, language is used as an important tool in teaching and learning. Through language, teachers communicate with students about the lesson content, administer discipline, manage interaction, create opportunities to learn and assess students' learning and performance. Similarly, children use language to communicate about the lesson content and to interact with the teacher and peers. Understanding the ways in which languages are used to teach and learn across the curriculum is an important part of understanding language in education.

Language in other academic subjects

Using language for teaching and learning within the institutional setting of schools emphasizes certain features of language and creates patterns of use which are different from the features and patterns of language used at home. Thus children need to learn to use language for educational purposes to be able to participate fully in the process of classroom learning. The language that students need to learn in school includes specialized vocabulary of curriculum subjects. Students need to learn many subject-specific terms and expressions, for which the connections between meanings and forms are mostly arbitrary. In science, for example, they have to learn *beaker, mass* and *evaporate*. Science teachers might think of these as important tools, concepts and processes but they are also vocabulary words with specific meanings in scientific contexts. Students must also learn how to manipulate grammatical structures of a language for specific uses in curriculum subjects. When using English to study mathematics, for example, students have to understand and use relative clauses (e.g. *the person who* . . .), comparatives (e.g. *more, most, greatest, least*) and other complex grammatical structures in order to do relatively simple mathematical calculations.

Students must also use language to explain ideas, construct arguments and describe events, things and people which are not in their immediate environment. For example, students might be studying about global water politics – an issue that may or may not be part of their daily lives. As part of their academic work on this topic, they would have to describe locations and situations, explain, summarize and synthesize information from different sources and argue from different points of view. In addition, students learn various educational conventions or ground rules of using language in school, for example, what is considered an appropriate way of bidding for a turn to answer the question the teacher asks or to ask the teacher a question. For children whose home language is different from the language used in school, they have to learn a new language or a new variety to be able to participate in these educational processes. Even those children whose home language is the same as the language used in school need to learn the differences between the spoken form of language used at home and the written texts they have to interpret and construct at school. They also learn about differences in conventions for literacy – types of reading and writing done at home (e.g. jotting down a grocery list) might not fit the conventions of reading and writing at school (e.g. writing a description in a composition).

To help students master the language requirements in educational settings and to achieve academic literacy, the teacher is crucial. The process and success of classroom education depends heavily not only on the language used by students but also the language used by teachers. For example, we have all had the experience, as students, of teacher explanations that didn't seem to explain much. And we are all likely as teachers to have the experience of giving a 'perfectly clear explanation' which somehow students did not follow. The specific language choices in an explanation can make a difference but so can the decision to give an example instead of an explanation – or to realize that words are not the best option and a visual would serve better. It is essential for teachers to have a fundamental grounding in what language is, how it is used in educational settings and the social implications of different types of interaction in the classroom. This is true in classes with students who share the same home-language background and in the ever-increasing number of classes with students who come from different language backgrounds or who have different levels of proficiency in the school language.

TEACHERS' AWARENESS OF LANGUAGE

In a well-known book, *Ways of Seeing*, John Berger states, 'The way we see things is affected by what we know or what we believe' (1972, p. 8). In order for teachers to see and understand what is happening with language in their classrooms, they must know more about language. They must also consider their own beliefs about language. **Language awareness** is a fundamental part of that seeing, knowing and believing. In fact, Stephen Andrews wrote an entire book on the importance on *Teacher Language Awareness*. Language is an underlying knowledge that teachers possess; this knowledge is not always explicit and teachers are not always consciously aware of their own language use. It is important for you to become more aware of how you use language to communicate in classrooms, how language can facilitate or impede learning and what your students need in terms of language learning and use. Some of the things that you need to be aware of are described briefly below.

- Language is made up of basic units which work together to create meanings.

Some units of language are, for example, sounds, morphemes, words, phrases and sentences. All languages have rules about how these units work together, so we say that language is 'rule-governed'. It is not enough to know the units, it is also essential to know the rules which allow the units to work together and how these create meanings. It is even possible to create new meanings by following the basic rules of a language. For example, if the student Nancy is supposed to clean the whiteboard in the classroom and forgets, the teacher might say, *Whiteboard, Nancy*. These two nouns with a small pause in between can be understood to mean *You need to clean the whiteboard, Nancy*. Subsequently the other students might turn this into a nickname *Whiteboard Nancy* using a 'rule' in English that lets nouns function as adjectives in some cases.

- Language is purposeful with embedded cultural and social meanings.

Language is used purposefully and those purposes include communication of different cultural and social meanings which are embedded in the way language is used. These differences can be within a language or across languages. In American English, for example, *excuse me* and *sorry* are both related to etiquette, unpleasantness and regret, but Ann Borkin and Susan Reinhart showed in 1978 that they function quite distinctly in different contexts. According to their work, *excuse me* is used for a breach in etiquette whether it just happened or is about to happen (e.g. after bumping into someone or when trying to push past someone in a crowded situation). *I'm sorry*, on the other hand, is used to express regret about something sad, unpleasant, disagreeable that has happened to the other person (e.g. *I'm sorry to hear you were sick and had to miss the concert*). Judging by online forums, this difference continues to bedevil those who are learning English as second language. It seems to be difficult for English speakers on different sides of the Atlantic Ocean to decide if *excuse me* is even needed! These differences are not based on issues of vocabulary and grammar but more on cultural and social rules for language use. How do teachers manage to use language effectively, especially in classes of students from different social, cultural and linguistic backgrounds?

- Every language has varieties.

Teachers must also be aware that there are different 'varieties' within a 'common' language, and speakers can have different ways of identifying themselves in relation to varieties. Different countries also have different policies about how those language varieties are used for education. These policies can be explicit (e.g. identifying the medium of instruction for schools) or implicit (e.g. an understanding that students learning Spanish will try to use only Spanish during class time).

- Processes of language learning are universal, but progress is unique to each individual.

Teachers need to be aware of some of the basic, universal processes of language development. Knowing some of these processes and common milestones of development can help teachers identify students who might need additional assistance. Although the processes of language learning are universal, each individual learns language uniquely so that he/she can be at different levels of proficiency for speaking, reading and writing (for example) and at different levels as compared with peers (perhaps better at reading as compared with peers, but weaker at speaking – or vice versa).

- Language learning and use at home and at school are not necessarily the same.

Equally important is being aware of some of the differences for language use at home and at school. Schools use language for educational purposes even when language is not the focus of study (e.g. even when studying physics or physical education instead of English or Chinese). Classroom language tends to follow particular patterns that may differ to language use in other contexts. Thus, learning to understand the 'code' of classroom talk is important whether the school language matches the home language or not.

As you might expect, the chapters in this book discuss each of these different areas of teacher language awareness in more detail.

INTENDED AUDIENCE AND PURPOSE OF THIS VOLUME

This volume is intended for those who are interested in the social implications of language in education. In particular, it is intended for prospective teachers (undergraduate or graduate) who are not specialists in linguistics or language learning, but who are interested in knowing more about how language is used, taught and learned in educational settings. The book can be used as essential or recommended reading for an introductory, teacher-training course at the undergraduate level. We have tried to make each chapter reader-friendly so it will appeal to those who are not specialists in language teaching or linguistics. We have also tried to cover essential, basic information on language in education so it can also be used as a foundational text for those who will be teaching language in the classroom. In addition, graduate students entering applied linguistics programmes but without a background in language and education will find that the book provides useful background information.

By putting together accessible explanations and discussions of some key features of language as well as important social implications of language use in educational settings, this volume aims to provide foundational knowledge on the roles of language in education. Although most programmes in Education or Applied Linguistics offer such courses as *Introduction to Language and Education* or *Language and Literacy*, few textbooks provide foundational knowledge on linguistics and a social view of language use in educational settings together in one book. Specifically, few books have presented an overview of the nature of language and its role in education for educators, or prospective educators, who are not language or linguistic specialists.

This volume introduces and addresses important issues on social implications of language use in educational settings, but it does not assume that you have a background in linguistics. The chapters included in this volume are carefully selected to provide you with a balanced introduction to technical issues related to foundational knowledge on linguistics (i.e. 'the linguistics end') and social implications of language (i.e. 'the social end') such as literacy, bilingual education and language policy. The chapters highlight key points related to the role of language in education. Many examples are included; where possible these come from a variety of international contexts. Through these examples, the chapters aim to provide opportunities for you to experience analysis of language and draw your own conclusions about how language is and can be used for educational purposes.

CHAPTER FORMAT

After this introductory chapter, there are eight key chapters in the book. Each chapter begins with an introduction to the topic, followed by accounts of several key issues and main discoveries in the topic area. A few key references are included; these will be useful to instructors and students who wish to read in more depth. Recommended reading and viewing are available at the end of each chapter and additional links to useful websites are also provided at the book's companion website www.bloomsbury.com/language-in-education-9781441151810 for those who want to read more broadly. Key terms are defined as they appear in each chapter. These terms are highlighted throughout the book using bold font. We also provide a glossary at the back of the book and at the companion website which covers all of the key terms.

In each chapter, discussions of key issues and relevance to educational settings or social implications are supported by examples. With readers of English as our audience, examples are predominantly in English but from international contexts. The chapters work with generalities that are appropriate for each topic, but highlight points, where necessary, that are specific to one language or one regional context/country. Chapters close with a set of questions which can be used for either in-class discussion or personal reflection.

OVERVIEW OF THE CHAPTERS

To help you understand the main focus of the individual chapters as well as the structure of the book overall, chapter summaries are provided here.

Chapter 2, by Lubna Alsagoff and Ho Chee Lick, provides necessary background on the 'units of language' and how language is structured. With a focus on the structure of English, the common language of our readers, the chapter gives teachers and prospective teachers the basic terminology, the most important concepts and the information necessary for thinking and talking about the structure of language knowledgeably.

In Chapter 3, Soe Marlar Lwin and Peter Teo address the ways in which language is used to make meaning in different contexts. The idea that language expresses meaning might seem quite self-evident but, as Lwin and Teo explain, to be able to use a language adequately and appropriately, we learn not only vocabulary and grammar but also how to use them for a purpose, how to convey that purpose to other users of the language and how to figure out the intended meaning which may not be transparent from the language form itself.

Chapter 4, by Anthea Fraser Gupta, takes the idea of variation in ways of using a language to express meaning a step further. The chapter examines some aspects of language varieties (i.e. variations in the pronunciation, spelling, grammar and vocabulary of a language) and discusses how they are linked to the regional origins and other social characteristics of language users.

Chapter 5, by Theres Grüter, addresses issues of language learning focusing on language acquisition in early childhood in a variety of learning situations, including monolingual and bilingual environments. Grüter explains how we know what 'normal' language development is and language development in children with language learning difficulties. Whether you are teaching children or adults, this background will give you a better understanding of the major social and cognitive factors that contribute to human language development.

Christine C. M. Goh and Paul Grahame Doyle introduce the key concepts of 'oracy' and 'literacy' in Chapter 6. They explain the ways spoken and written language support each other in a person's language development and language use. The influence that family practices have on children's oracy and literacy development and the role of teachers' oral communication in class in children's development of disciplinary literacies are also discussed.

Chapter 7, by Rita Elaine Silver, Raslinda A. R. and Galyna Kogut, deals with language in educational contexts, in particular with common patterns of classroom interaction – patterns which seem to transcend different countries and different languages. The chapter introduces how language is used in study across academic subjects and explains the different ways teachers can use talk in the classroom, including pros and cons of different types of teacher talk. Different types of student talk and ways in which they can impact student learning are also addressed.

In Chapter 8, Manka M. Varghese and Rukmini Becerra Lubies go into more detail about issues for learners who do not use the school language as their home language – or perhaps learners have multiple languages and the school language is only one of several languages they use in daily life. They talk about different definitions of bilingual and bilingualism and explain the advantages of viewing bilinguals holistically. They also review some of the benefits of being bilingual. The idea of language proficiencies and of different proficiencies for different languages and different language skills are also discussed.

In Chapter 9, Francis M. Hult introduces the idea of language policy and the implications of language policy for educational contexts and educators. He explores the different scales of society, ranging from governments to schools and classrooms, where educational policy and planning are shaped. His chapter specifically addresses ideas of teachers as policy implementers and policymakers as they constantly work with language in educational contexts.

The individual chapters stand alone and, thus, do not have to be read in the order given. However, attention has been paid to cross-referencing information so you will be aware when different chapters have related information.

DISCUSSION AND REFLECTION QUESTIONS

1   At the beginning of the chapter, we write about *the nature of language* and say that human language is different from animal communication in at least four ways. One of these ways is productivity. Re-read the explanation in the book and think of at least three examples of productivity in human language.

2   Based on what you have read in this chapter or your own experiences and ideas, try to think of three ways in which 'language awareness' is important for teachers even if they are not language teachers.

3   In this chapter, we say *language learning and use at home and at school are not necessarily the same*. Can you think of any examples from your own life?

RECOMMENDED READING AND VIEWING

Wikipedia has a decent summary of issues around animal communication, including links to information about Charles Hockett and others who work in this line of research. See:

   http://en.wikipedia.org/wiki/Animal_language

Mark Pagel, a biologist, gives a fascinating talk on TED talks in which he explains his view of the role of language in human evolution. Whether or not you accept his point of view on that, he gives an excellent explanation of the social implications of language. See:

   http://www.ted.com/talks/lang/en/mark_pagel_how_language_ transformed_humanity.html

An online article by Jay focuses on children using profanity and possible adult responses. Beyond that, it is a useful discussion of differences in home/ school language, family values around language and managing children's language behaviour.

   Jay, T. (2007), 'When young children use profanity: How to handle cursing and name calling'. *EarlychildhoodNEWS*. Excelligence Learning Corporation. Available at: www.earlychildhoodnews.com/earlychildhood/ article_print.aspx?ArticleId=59

Some of the research details in the article by Catherine Snow and her colleagues might be more than you want to know. However, the information about 'the tasks and materials' used for language assessment is very useful. (See the section on 'methods'.) These can help you think about how different kinds of tasks provide different kinds of evidence of language knowledge.

Snow, S. E., Tabors, P. O., Nicholson, P. A. and Kurland, B. F. (1995), 'SHELL: Oral language and early literacy skills in kindergarten and first-grade children'. *Journal of Research on Childhood Education,* 10, 37–48.

As mentioned in the chapter, Stephen Andrews has written a book about language teacher awareness. It is specifically for language teachers and second language teachers, but it has useful information for everyone who teaches in classroom contexts.

Andrews, S. (2007), *Teacher Language Awareness.* Cambridge: Cambridge University Press.

2

What Is the Structure of Language?

Lubna Alsagoff and Ho Chee Lick

INTRODUCTION

Language is a semiotic system. By this we mean that it is a set of signs used to convey meaning. There are many semiotic systems that we encounter in our everyday lives, for example, traffic lights signal information to us through changes in lights. Language differs from these other semiotic systems in its complexity. In particular, the 'design features' of human language (see Chapter 1) enable it to serve as a highly versatile means of communication in a wide range of contexts. For example, language allows us to convey information about things that happened in the past, and the number of sentences that users of a language can produce, and comprehend, is vast if not infinite!

Although the range of language signs is so vast, all of these signs, at the lowest level, are made up of combinations from an inventory of speech sounds (or if we think about writing, it can be seen as being composed of symbols that represent sound). These sounds combine to form words. For example, the word *pits* consists of four sounds: /p/, /ɪ/, /t/ and /s/. We study the sounds of a language in the branch of linguistics known as phonetics.

If we examine the word *pits* more closely, we find that it is in fact composed of two different parts: *pit* and *s*. These parts are units of meaning known as morphemes, and we study the way in which morphemes combine to form words in a branch of linguistics known as morphology. A closely related field of study is syntax, which studies the way words combine to form sentences. Together, the sub-disciplines of morphology and syntax are referred to as grammar. Finally, in any study of the structure of language, we examine how words convey meaning either by themselves or when combined to form phrases and sentences – this is the branch of linguistics known as semantics.

In this chapter, we will focus on the basic concepts which will be helpful for future teachers. As the chapter spans four very important branches of linguistics (phonetics, morphology, syntax and semantics), we will only be able to discuss basic concepts and ideas. Many of the explanations have been simplified for this introductory overview. It is also impossible to cover many of the structural differences across languages in this one chapter. Therefore, our focus is on the structure of English, the common language of our readers, and our examples are drawn from that language.

PHONETICS

We begin with **phonetics**, the study of speech sounds. There are three different approaches to phonetics. We can study:

- how speech sounds are produced (articulatory phonetics),
- their physical characteristics (acoustic phonetics) and
- how speech sounds are perceived (auditory phonetics).

In this chapter, we will be focusing only on articulatory phonetics as this is the most useful area of phonetics for teachers.

An important aspect of studying phonetics is to have a set of technical terms to discuss the sounds of speech, as well as a way to represent the sounds of English. To be able to study, discuss and write about speech sounds in language, linguists use a phonetic alphabet. A phonetic alphabet is different from an orthographic or writing alphabet. Whereas the latter is about spelling a written word, the former is about how to accurately and consistently represent speech sounds. The most commonly used phonetic alphabet is **International Phonetic Alphabet (IPA)** which we use in this chapter.

A phonetic alphabet is especially useful in talking about a language like English which has high levels of inconsistency between the spelling of words and their pronunciation. For example, although the following words *leaf*, *off*, *calf*, *giraffe*, *enough*, *graph* are each spelt with a different ending, they all in fact end with the same sound, which can be represented in the IPA as /f/. Conversely, although the words, *such*, *hubs* and *pleasure* all contain the letter *s*, each of the *s*'s is in fact different in pronunciation. The use of the IPA allows us to represent the different sounds of the *s* spelling as distinct: /s/ in *such*, /z/ in *hubs* and /ʒ/ in *pleasure*.

The IPA is a universal alphabet – it contains symbols for describing speech sounds not just in English but other languages as well. Thus, having a universal phonetic alphabet gives linguists, teachers and those who are involved in the study of speech a means of talking about different sounds very specifically, for any language. The IPA, along with the set of technical descriptors which we describe below in the subsections on consonants and vowels, can also be used to identify dialectal variations in pronunciation (see Chapter 4) as well as diagnose speech production problems.

Articulation of speech sounds

Human beings have highly developed vocal organs. Producing a speech sound might seem effortless, but the process is a highly complex one, as we will shortly see.

In English, all speech sounds begin with air being forced outwards from the lungs. The air travels upwards through the vocal or 'articulatory tract', which we illustrate in Figure 2.1. The air first passes through the larynx, which

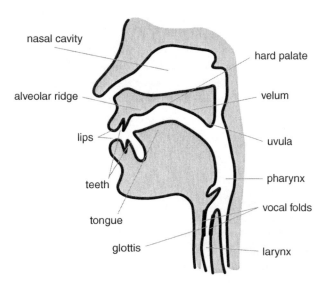

FIGURE 2.1 *The articulatory tract*

contains the vocal folds. In many men, we can see where the vocal folds are; they appear as a bump at the front of the neck – what is often referred to as the 'Adam's apple'. As the air flows through the opening between the vocal folds, called the 'glottis', it begins to take on different qualities, depending on the position of the vocal folds, especially whether they vibrate. There are two important contrastive positions for the vocal folds:

- When the vocal folds are held loosely together, they vibrate as air passes through the glottis. These vibrations (technically known as 'phonation') produce 'voiced' sounds. Pitch is also a result of this vibration, rising or falling depending on how fast the vocal folds are vibrating. Vowels are voiced sounds as are some consonants, for example, the first sound of the following words: /z/ as in *zoo*, /b/ as in *b*it and /dʒ/ as in *J*ill.

- When the vocal folds are held wide apart, the glottis is open, and air passes through it freely. The sounds that are produced are 'voiceless' sounds. This is also the normal position of the vocal folds when we are breathing. Consonants are sounds such as /s/ as in *s*ue, /p/ as in *p*it and /tʃ/ as in *ch*ill.

Photographs of the two positions of the vocal folds can be found at www. departments.bucknell.edu/linguistics/lectures/glottis.jpg.

From the pharyngeal cavity, air now flows into the most important part of the vocal tract, the mouth or oral cavity. This space is intricately shaped by various articulators in the mouth, such as the lips, tongue, teeth, alveolar (teeth) ridge and palate, which determine the characteristics of the speech sounds. The lips and tongue are particularly important in blocking off air, and shaping the way the air moves through the vocal tract. Although air passes through the oral cavity in the production of most speech sounds, it can also pass through the nose or nasal cavity. When the velum (soft palate) at the back of the oral cavity is in a lowered position, air can pass through the nasal cavity – this produces nasal sounds like the *m*'s and *n*'s that you hear in words like *mum* and *noon*.

Speech sounds of English

Languages use different sets of speech sounds to form words to convey meanings. For example, English meaningfully differentiates a sound produced by the two lips, /p/ and one that uses the lower lip and teeth, /f/. This means that English speakers will hear and understand /fɪn/ *fin* and /pɪn/ *pin* as two different words. In contrast, many varieties of Malay do not distinguish the two sounds, /p/ and /f/, and it is therefore possible to say a Malay word like *faham* (to understand) with a /p/ or a /f/ at the beginning of the word without any change of meaning.

Speech sounds can be classified into consonants or vowels depending on the way they are produced. Consonants are defined as sounds which are produced by obstructing the airflow in some manner along the vocal tract. Different consonants are produced by varying the place of the stricture and the manner in which the airflow is obstructed and released through the stricture. Consonants can also vary depending on whether or not the vocal folds vibrate in producing the speech sound. Vowels, on the other hand, are sounds which are produced without any obstruction in the articulatory tract; instead how they sound depends on the way the tongue and lips shape the articulatory tract.

Consonants

Consonants are described by using three features:

- Place of articulation: This is the point in the oral tract where the air flow is obstructed. In describing the place of articulation for consonants, we use the articulators as points of reference. For example, a sound like /p/ is described as bilabial because it is produced by putting the upper lip and lower lip together; /f/, on the other hand, is described as a labiodental sound because the lower lip (labio-) comes into contact with the teeth (dental).

- Manner of articulation: This describes how the air is obstructed and how it is released. There are different ways in which the air flow can be obstructed. For example, sounds like /p/, /t/, /k/ involve the airflow being blocked completely and then released suddenly, resulting in consonants which we call 'plosives'. In contrast, a sound like /s/ is where the air flow is not blocked off completely, but rather released slowly through a small opening, causing friction. Another way to vary the manner of articulation is to lower the velum, allowing air to pass through the nasal cavity (nasal) or oral cavity.

- Voicing: This describes whether the vocal folds are vibrating. When the vocal folds are vibrating, voiced sounds are produced; if they are not vibrating, voiceless consonants are produced. In English, there are many contrastive pairs of consonants which are produced in the same place and manner, but differ in terms of voicing. Some examples include /p/ and /b/, /t/ and /d/, /s/ and /z/ where the first consonant is voiceless and the second one is voiced.

If we combine these three elements, we can say, for example, that /p/ is a voiceless bilabial plosive, whereas /b/ is a voiced bilabial plosive.

Vowels

Vowels are speech sounds for which there is no obstruction to the flow of air through the oral cavity. There are two kinds of vowels. Words such as *pit, pet, putt, pot, put* contain pure vowels or **monophthongs**, whereas words like *pike, pay, pound* contain **diphthongs** or glides. Monophthongs are produced with the tongue in a single position, whereas diphthongs are formed when the tongue moves from one position to another, thus producing a glide. Diphthongs generally sound as if they comprise two vowels that are said one after another.

To describe a (pure) vowel, we use the following features:

- Length of vowel: A vowel is either long or short, for example, *sheep ~ ship*; *pool ~ pull*.

- The height of the tongue body: We usually distinguish between an open, mid and close vowel, for example, *bard ~ bad ~ bid*, depending on how raised the tongue body is.

- The front-back position of the tongue: We classify sounds depending on whether the sound is made with the tongue raised at the front, middle or back of the mouth. For example, the vowel in *bid* is a front vowel, while the vowel for *bird* is a central vowel and that of *bored* is a back vowel.

- Whether lips are rounded or not: In articulating vowels, whether the lips are rounded or not makes a difference to the way the vowel sounds. Vowels like those in *shoot, shot, school, pot* are all made with rounded lips whereas the vowels in words such as *lift, leaf, lap, laugh, hurt, heart* are made with unrounded lips.

In this short section, we have discussed a small part of the study of phonetics. We looked at the way in which speech sounds are produced, and discussed how the speech sounds are described with reference to the vocal organs used to produce them.

MORPHOLOGY

From the study of sounds, we move to the study of words and how they are formed. In the study of word formation or **morphology**, we can start with a simple observation that many words which we use in everyday life are made up of even smaller parts. Take the words, *trees, warned, smaller, development, homeless* and *untidy*. These are in fact made up of smaller components, known as **morphemes**: *tree+s, warn+ed, small+er, develop+ment, home+less* and *un+tidy*.

Let's look at two of the most common ways in which words can be formed by combining morphemes. The first is **affixation**, and the second, **compounding**.

Affixation

In word formation, there are morphemes which cannot stand alone as words. These morphemes, known as **affixes**, are added on to words. Affixes which attach to the front of a word are known as prefixes, while those that attach to the back of words are known as suffixes. There are two kinds of affixation. The first is known as **inflection**, in which affixation produces a variant form of the same word. The second is **derivation**, in which affixation changes one word into a different, although related, word – the new word has either a different word class or may differ in meaning from the original word.

Inflection

Let us look at three examples of inflection from the list of words we began with:

- The word *tree+s* is a noun, *tree*, with an *-s* suffix (or ending), which marks it as plural, that is 'more than one'. We can form the plurals of countable nouns in this regular way: *dogs, roofs, leaves, enemies, buses* and *benches*.

- There is, likewise, a regular way in which we can indicate when a verb is in the past tense, by adding an *-ed* at the end of a verb: *warn+ed*. Examples of other verbs which are of this pattern: *melted, earned, obeyed, remembered, carried* and *confirmed*.

- The word *small+er* is the comparative form of the adjective *small*, in which the *-er* suffix is added to it. Words such as *older, happier, weaker, tougher* and *purer* are formed in this manner.

In each of these examples of inflection, notice that the suffix produces a variant form of the same word. *Tree* and *trees* are considered to be the same noun, with *tree+s* being its plural form. *Warn* and *warned* are the same verb, with *warn+ed* being its past tense form. *Small* and *smaller* are the same adjective, with *small+er* being its comparative form.

One important point to note in these examples is that some of the plurals, past tense or comparative forms may have special ways of spelling or pronunciation, for example, *leaf/leaves, enemy/enemies, fry/fried, grin/grinned, pure/purer, happy/happier*, etc. These changes in spelling or pronunciation do not change the fundamental meaning of the word. There are a number of plurals or past tense words that are not formed through regular inflections. These irregular forms include *child/children, man/men* (plural); *win/won, lie/lay* (past tense).

Derivation

The formation patterns of *develop+ment, home+less, quiet+ly* and *un+tidy* represent a different kind of affixation called derivation, in which affixes are used to form a different word.

- The word *develop+ment* is formed by adding the *-ment* suffix to the verb *develop*, to produce a different word, *development*. The suffix, *-ment*, produces an abstract noun with the meaning 'action, process or result of . . .'. There are many other nouns that can be formed using the suffix *-ment*, for example, *achievement, commitment, involvement* and *retirement*.

- The word *home+less* is formed by adding the suffix *-less* to the noun *home*, to produce an adjective, *homeless*. Other words formed in this way include: *clueless, jobless, friendless, leafless* and *bottomless*.

- And in *untidy*, the prefix *un-* is added to an adjective *tidy*, to produce another adjective with a general meaning that means the opposite of the base adjective. Other adjectives produced in the same way include *unconscious, unable, uncommon* and *unequal*.

In these three examples, we see that derivation differs from inflection in a number of ways. While inflection makes use of only a handful of suffixes, namely, -s for 'countable' noun; -s, -ing, -ed for regular verbs; -er, -est for gradable adjectives, derivation involves a very much larger number of suffixes:

> digit+al; free+dom; employ+ee; teach+er; sharp+en; peace+ful; hero+ic; class+ify; protect+ion; standard+ize; child+ish; art+ist; stupid+ity; attract+ive; fair+ness; music+ology; friend+ship; trouble+some; sky+ward; greed+y

In addition, unlike inflection, derivation can make use of prefixes. Prefixes can be added to the various word classes, for example, nouns (N), verbs (V), adjectives (A) to substantially change the meaning of words:

> sub+N: subcontinent; subsection
>
> non+N: non-member; non-fiction
>
> mini+N: minibus; mini-camera
>
> re+V: rebuild; reappear
>
> dis+V: disobey; discontinue
>
> mis+V: misinform; mispronounce
>
> un+A: unhappy; untrue
>
> in+A: inaccurate; insane
>
> semi+A: semiconscious; semirural

They can also result in a word belonging to a different word class:

> en+A: enlarge; enable (changing an adjective into a verb)
>
> de+N: debone; deforest (changing a noun into a verb)
>
> pro+N: pro-democracy; pro-war (changing a noun into an adjective)

Another interesting difference between derivation and inflection is that inflection can only be applied once in the formation of a word, whereas derivational affixation can be used recursively to form larger and larger words. Take the word non-renewable, for instance; it can be analysed as involving three steps of derivational affixation:

> new (A)
> Step 1: re+new (V 'to make new again')
> Step 2: renew+able (A 'can be renewed')
> Step 3: non+renewable (A 'cannot be renewed')

Compounding

Another way in which words are formed is through **compounding**, in which two (or more) words are combined to form a different word. For example, the word *dead+line*, meaning 'a specific date or time by which one has to do or complete something', is made up of two component parts *dead* and *line*, both of which can be used independently as words.

Below are some typical examples of compounding, listed according to the word class of the whole compound word.

Compound nouns:

highway ('a wide main road that joins cities or towns together')

party animal ('a person who enjoys going to lots of parties')

make-believe ('fanciful pretence')

Compound verbs:
shoplift ('to steal goods on display in a shop')

pinpoint ('to discover, locate, identify or explain with precision')

bad-mouth ('to say unpleasant things about someone or something')

Compound adjectives:
homesick ('unhappy because of being far from home for a long period')

true-blue ('completely loyal' or 'genuine')

well off ('rich')

From these examples we can see that compounding is much more complex than affixation (inflection and derivation). It is much more difficult, for example, to determine the meaning of a compound word from its component words. Such issues are, however, beyond the scope of our current chapter.

We will use a simple figure to sum up our discussion on morphology (see Figure 2.2).

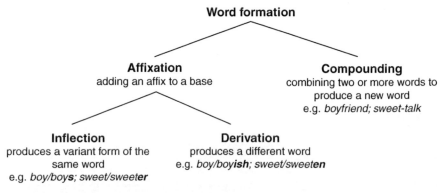

FIGURE 2.2 *Word formation processes*

SYNTAX

We now turn our attention to the way in which words combine to form sentences. This is commonly referred to as the study of **syntax**.

Words and phrases

When we speak or write, we use words and combine them to form sentences. However, a sentence is not formed by simply stringing individual words one after another into a line. Instead, words are first combined to form larger structural units called phrases, and then phrases are used as constituents for sentence construction. Thus, if we analyse the sentence, structural units called phrases, and then phrases are used as constituents for sentence construction. Thus, if we analyse the sentence, *His sister has packed some clean shirts in his suitcase*, we find that the ten words are first grouped into four phrases, as indicated by the brackets:

   [His sister] [has packed] [some clean shirts] [in his suitcase].

Phrases behave as units. As such, phrases are moveable as a whole. Notice, for example, that *in his suitcase* can be moved as a unit to the front of the sentence:

   [In his suitcase] his sister has packed some clean shirts [   ].

We cannot, in contrast, move words that do not form a unit. We mark what is grammatically incorrect with an asterisk, *.

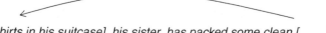

   *[Shirts in his suitcase] his sister has packed some clean [   ].

In addition to being able to move phrases around, we can also substitute phrases with single words such as pronouns or question words. For example, *some clean shirts* can be substituted by the pronoun *them*:

   His sister has packed [them] in his suitcase.

We can also use *who* to substitute for the phrase *his sister*:

   [Who] has packed some clean shirts in his suitcase?

From these examples, we note that not all groupings of words can form phrases. Let's start by comparing what can, and what cannot, be a grammatically well-formed phrase. If we take the same three words *some, clean* and *shirts* again, we note that there are six different ways to put them together, but only one way results in a well-formed phrase in English (Table 2.1).

TABLE 2.1 Noun phrases

Well-formed noun phrase	Ill-formed noun phrases
some clean shirts	**clean some shirts*
	*some shirts clean
	*shirts some clean
	*clean shirts some
	*shirt clean some

This clearly shows us that there is a specific word order for this particular kind of phrase. In addition, we note that it is a phrase that is formed around the noun *shirts*, with *some* and *clean* as additional (i.e. optional) words that give us more information about it. For this reason, we refer to such phrases as 'noun phrases', and refer to the noun, *shirts*, as the 'head' of the phrase. In English, words such as determiners (e.g. *the, that, some* and *many*) and adjectives (e.g. *clean, beautiful, white* and *expensive*) are said to modify the head. Note that these appear before the noun, with determiners appearing before adjectives. For this reason, we refer to them as premodifiers of the head noun.

We can represent the structure of a noun phrase as:

noun phrase	→	(determiner)	+	(adjective)	+	noun
		some		*clean*		*shirts*

Here we indicate optional elements of the noun phrase through the use of parentheses. Note that only the head of the noun phrase is obligatory. By combining these different classes of words, we can form an endless variety of noun phrases, for example, *a crazy fellow, my favourite song, that new library, many possible solutions*. As we explore noun phrases further, we will, of course, find that the structure is far more complex, and that the rule we have just stated needs to be expanded to take into account these more complex structures. In particular, apart from premodifiers, noun phrases can also contain postmodifiers – these are groups of words that modify the head noun, but which follow rather than precede it.

Notice that in describing the structure of the noun phrase, we used terms like 'noun', 'adjective' and 'determiner' to indicate the different classes of words that are involved in the construction of a noun phrase. Intuitively, we know that words like *teacher, shirt* and *library* are similar in terms of their meaning: They name people, things or places. Similarly, we can group words such as *happy, clean* and *favourite* under one word class because these are words that generally describe people, things or places.

Word class, however, is not only about distinguishing meaning. It has to do, more importantly, with distinguishing the different ways in which words behave in terms of where and how they can be used in a sentence, as well as the different forms they can take. For instance, words like *the, those, your, any* and *enough* are categorized as determiners on the basis that they precede, rather than follow, the adjective(s) before the head noun in the noun phrase structure, as we observed above. Earlier in the section on morphology, we saw that many word classes such as noun and verb are also identifiable by their word formation patterns, for example, a noun like *shirt* can take a plural form, *shirts*. In English, we generally recognize eight different word classes (Table 2.2).

TABLE 2.2 English word classes

Word class	Examples	Definition
Noun	*student, door, library, freedom*	typically refers to people, things, places or ideas
Verb	*write, live, seem*	typically refers to actions or states of being
Adjective	*tall, shiny, strong*	typically describes people, things, places and ideas
Adverb	*immediately, quietly*	typically describes actions
Pronoun	*she, him, I, me, you*	typically stands in place of a noun
Preposition	*on, in, under*	relates two noun phrases to each other, typically in space or time, as in *the book on the table*
Conjunction	*and, but, because*	joins words, or phrases, or sentences together
Determiner	*a, the, this, that, these, those, his, her, their*	combines word classes such as articles, demonstratives and possessives which introduce a noun, typically by pointing to the person/thing that is being talked about

You should be aware that descriptions of the grammar of English often differ in the way they classify word classes. Some grammar references, for example, might decide to recognize quantifiers such as *five, twenty, some, few* and *many* as a type of adjective. Some other grammars might choose to refer to many other categories of words as separate word classes, for example, articles and demonstratives, rather than group them together as determiners. Grammars that wish to describe spoken language might include interjectives as the ninth word class – this is the class of words like *gosh, alas, wow*, which express emotions.

To complete our discussion on the way words combine to form phrases, we want to highlight that the way in which phrases are formed can be complex. For example, the preposition phrase, *in his suitcase*, comprises a two-level phrase structure:

$$\left\{ in\ [\ his\ suitcase\ ] \right\}$$

We can also represent this embedded structure by drawing what is known as a phrase structure 'tree' diagram (Figure 2.3):

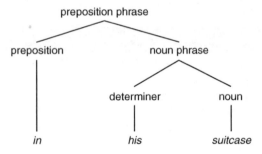

FIGURE 2.3 *A phrase structure 'tree' diagram*

These two different representations show that there are two levels of phrase structure. At the 'lower' level, we see that the noun *suitcase* combines with the determiner *his* to form a noun phrase, *his suitcase*. At the 'higher' level, this noun phrase combines with the preposition *in* to form a preposition phrase, *in his suitcase*.

What is important to note is that a phrase (the noun phrase) can be used as a component part within another phrase (the prepositional phrase). In fact, preposition phrases can again be used as a component part within another phrase. This provides further evidence that we do not simply string one word after another to form a sentence. Instead, we see that words are grouped together in structural units called phrases which are then used at different levels or embedded to form larger and more complex structural units.

Sentence structure

Just as there are many ways to put words together to form phrases, so are there also many different ways we can use and combine phrases to form different sentence structures. In English, depending on the main verb that is used, sentences can take one of five basic sentence structures (Table 2.3).

TABLE 2.3 Basic English sentence structures

	[The prisoner]	[disappeared].		
1	Subject	Verb		
	[My brother]	[was]	[hungry].	
2	Subject	Verb	Complement	
	[My teacher]	[received]	[a letter].	
3	Subject	Verb	Object	
	[My mother]	[gave]	[the woman]	[a book].
4	Subject	Verb	Indirect Object	Direct Object
	[My uncle]	[urged]	[my aunt]	[to travel].
5	Subject	Verb	Object	Object Complement

Languages differ in the way they sequence the **grammatical functions** of Subject, Verb and Object to form a sentence. English has a fairly fixed word order – it is known as an SVO language because its grammatical functions usually appear with the Subject followed by the Verb, which is then followed by the Object. Other languages such as Greek or Norwegian, which English is historically related to, also have this word order. There are other unrelated languages such as Swahili, Mandarin and Malay which are also SVO languages. In contrast, languages such as Japanese, Turkish, Latin and German, to name a few, are called SOV languages because their Objects typically come before their Verbs in sentences. Most languages in the world are either SVO or SOV in their word order.

Let us examine one of the sentence structures of English, Subject + Verb + Object, in greater detail to understand the ways in which phrases can play different roles or functions in a sentence:

The students have submitted their assignments.

	[The students]	[have submitted]	[their assignments].
Phrase:	noun phrase	verb group	noun phrase
Function:	Subject	Verb	Object

Note that we have referred to the phrase *have submitted* as a verb group rather than a verb phrase because many linguists use the term 'verb phrase' to refer to the string of verbs as well as the components that follow it, that is, *have submitted their assignment*. And we use the term 'Verb' that begins with a capital letter, to refer to the grammatical function of the verb group.

When phrases are combined to form a sentence, they each have a particular role or function to play. Just as words such as adjectives and nouns play the roles of premodifiers or heads in noun phrases, so do phrases play a role or function in the structure of a sentence. Thus, even though there are two noun phrases in the above sentence, their grammatical functions are different in relation to the verb group. The grammatical function of the first noun phrase, *the students*, is the Subject of the sentence, while the second noun phrase, *their assignments*, is the Object. Typically, the Subject occurs before the Verb, while the Object occurs after it. In terms of meaning, Subject is usually associated with the 'agent' – the one responsible for doing the action, while the Object is associated with the 'patient' – the one the action is performed on.

The students have submitted their assignments.

	[The students]	[have submitted]	[their assignments].
Meaning:	agent	process	patient
Function:	Subject	Verb	Object

We can, however, change this meaning association by making the sentence *passive*:

The assignments have been submitted (by the students).

	[The assignments]	[have been submitted].
Meaning:	patient	process
Function:	Subject	Verb

In the passive sentence, the Subject is no longer the agent of the action; instead, the patient becomes the Subject. Note that the agent in the passive sentence *by the students* is optional and can be left out. In fact, passive sentences are especially useful in writing when we are not certain who carried out the action or when we wish to highlight the patient.

It is thus important to distinguish between the different grammatical functions in a sentence because grammatical functions help determine the structure of many grammatical constructions. We give two further illustrations below.

i   Subject-Verb Agreement

Notice that the verb group of a sentence must always *agree in number* with the noun phrase which functions as its Subject.

The students have submitted their assignments.

| *[The students]* | *[have (*has) submitted]* | *[their assignments].* |
| Subject | Verb | Object |

If the Subject noun phrase is plural, then the verb group must also be plural, as in the example above. If we change the Subject to a singular noun phrase, as we see below, the verb group must correspondingly be changed to the singular:

The student has submitted her assignments.

| *[The student]* | *[has (*have) submitted]* | *[her assignments].* |
| Subject | Verb | Object |

Notice that agreement does not depend on the Object. So even when the Object, *her assignments*, is plural, the verb group still remains singular.

ii   Pronoun Case

The **case** of a noun or pronoun refers to the different forms they take depending on their grammatical function in a phrase or sentence. In English only pronouns have case. For example, if we use the first person pronoun in the Subject position, we need to use *I*. In contrast, when we use the first person pronoun as the Object or Complement of a sentence, we need to use *me*.

| *I* | *like* | *the photographs.* |
| Subject | Verb | Object |

| *The photographer* | *followed* | *me.* |
| Subject | Verb | Object |

| *That man in the hat* | *is* | *me.* |
| Subject | Verb | Complement |

Most of the pronouns in English have different forms for the subjective and objective cases (Table 2.4).

TABLE 2.4 Pronoun case

Subjective form	Objective form
I	*me*
he	*him*
she	*her*
we	*us*
they	*them*

Returning to our example sentence, if we wanted to use a pronoun to substitute *the students*, we would use the (subjective) pronoun *they*, rather than the (objective) pronoun *them*.

[The students]	[have submitted]	[their assignments].
[They (*Them)]	[have submitted]	[their assignments].
Subject	Verb	Object

The objective case is also required in prepositional phrases – the pronoun after the preposition must be in the objective form:

The students submitted their assignments	*[to the teacher].*
The students submitted their assignments	*[to her *(she)].*

In our discussion on syntax in this section, we have addressed three issues in examining how sentences are formed: We learnt that phrases, rather than words, are the constituents of sentence formation; we then looked at examples of how phrases are formed, and how their structures can be represented by rules, bracketing structures and phrase structure trees. We also looked at the ways in which phrases take on different syntactic functions in a sentence.

SEMANTICS

We have seen how sounds make up words which in turn make up phrases and sentences. Phonetics, morphology and syntax are the study of structures whereas our final topic, semantics, which is the study of meaning, is quite different. Interestingly, individual speech sounds have no meaning, so we can't ask what each of the sounds, /p/, / ɪ /, /t/ or /s/ means, but when we combine them in specific ways, the sounds form words that have meaning, for example /pɪts/, /spɪt/. Words in turn, as we have seen, combine to form phrases, which in turn form sentences.

Semantics can be explored at different levels – we can examine meaning at the word-level, sentence-level or even at the text-level. To give you a quick insight into some of the ways meaning can be studied, we will examine three basic topics in semantics: synonyms, ambiguity and meaning connection between sentences (see also Chapter 3).

Synonyms

Within the vocabulary, or what is more technically called the lexicon of a language, word meanings are interrelated in a variety of ways. As a simple example, consider the meaning relation between *joy, happiness, sorrow* and *emotion*. *Joy* and *happiness* have basically the same meaning; while *joy* and *sorrow* have opposite meanings; *joy* and *sorrow* are types of *emotion*. Semanticists have studied these and other types of meaning relations between words.

Let us take a closer look at the meaning relation between the two words *joy* and *happiness*. Words such as these, which have the same or nearly the same meaning, are technically referred to as **synonyms**; their meaning relation is synonymy. Here are some familiar examples: *sick ~ ill, almost ~ nearly, begin ~ start, buy ~ purchase, thoughtful ~ considerate, intentional ~ deliberate*.

Synonyms do not have to come in pairs and can also be applied to set phrases, that is words that are commonly used together, such as *by and large*, and *to do away with* as well.

> *enough ~ adequate ~ sufficient*
> *estimate ~ appraise ~ evaluate ~ assess ~ rate*
> *discard ~ get rid of ~ dispose of ~ do away with*
> *generally speaking ~ in general ~ by and large ~ for the most part*

It should be pointed out that perfect synonymy is very rare. Most synonyms are near synonyms – although they might be very similar in meaning, there is some difference between them:

> *Commence* and *begin* mean practically the same thing, but *commence* is a much more formal word than *begin*.
> *Ladies and gentlemen, we may now commence/begin the meeting.*
> *Hi guys, it's time to begin (*commence) our warm-up game!*

Agony and *pain* both mean 'physical or mental suffering'; *agony* however is a much stronger word than *pain*, suggesting 'pain that is too intense to bear'.
The most common technique to reduce the pain (*agony) of an injection is simply to distract the patient.

Chuckle and *snigger* both mean 'laughing quietly'; they differ in that *snigger* is a negative word with an element of 'unkindness' – for example, laughing at someone's problems or mistakes.
I couldn't stop chuckling (*sniggering) when my best friend showed me his baby photos.
When the bully spilled coffee all over his trousers, we all sniggered (*chuckled).

Although dictionaries are a good resource to find out what words mean, they often do not define these more subtle aspects of word meaning which might cause problems for learners.

Another point worth mentioning is that synonyms are usually quite different in terms of what words they collocate with, that is what words they usually occur with. Consider *danger* and *risk*. They have the same meaning 'the possibility of something bad happening'. We can use them interchangeably as in *to increase the danger/risk of*, or *to pose a real danger/ risk*. However, there are specific words that only one, but not the other, can go together with, for example, *to take the risk (*danger) of, to have a high risk (*danger) of, to be in danger (*risk), to be at risk (*danger).*

Ambiguity

Simply put, when something said or written can have two or more different meanings, we say that it is ambiguous. **Ambiguity** is different from vagueness which means that we are not able to discern the meaning of something.

Have you found the bat? is ambiguous, because *bat* can mean 'a flying mouse-like animal' or 'a specially shaped wooden club for hitting the ball in games like cricket or baseball'. These two meanings come, in fact, from two unrelated words – *bat* (an animal) and *bat* (a wooden club) – which just happen to be pronounced and spelt the same way.

Similarly, the sentence *We have agreed to build more bridges between our two countries* is also ambiguous, due to the two possible meanings of *bridge*: 'a structure built over a river, etc.' and 'something which provides an (abstract) connection between two things'. But in this case, the two different meanings can be seen as coming from one and the same word *bridge*: The abstract meaning of *bridge* as a 'connection' is a metaphorical extension of the more basic, concrete meaning of *bridge* as a 'structure'.

When ambiguity arises from the various meanings of one (or more) of the words in the sentence, we refer to it as **lexical ambiguity**. However, if a sentence is ambiguous not because of any particular word(s), but because the words it contains can be grouped/structured in different ways, resulting in different interpretations, we say that this is a matter of **structural ambiguity**.

Consider the sentence, *He accidentally hit the man with the umbrella*. It can be interpreted as either 'he was using an umbrella and he accidentally hit the man with it' or 'he accidentally hit the man who was carrying an umbrella'. These two totally different meanings come not from any ambiguous word, but from two possible, different ways of structuring the words that make up the sentence. In the first interpretation, the preposition phrase, *with the umbrella,* is structurally related to the verb *hit*; that is, it modifies the verb, describing how, or with what instrument, the action was accomplished. In the second interpretation, the preposition phrase, *with the umbrella,* is structurally related to the noun *man*; that is, it postmodifies the noun, and describes which man (i.e. the man with the umbrella and not, for example, the man with the guitar) was hit.

Let's look at yet another example. In the sentence *They promised to pay us in May*, the preposition phrase *in May* can be structurally related either to the verb *promised*, describing when the promise was made (with no mention of the payment time), or to the verb *to pay*, indicating when the payment would be made (with no mention of the time the promise was made). These two structuring possibilities thus render the sentence ambiguous.

Our above discussion focuses on how the language, as a system, allows lexical and structural ambiguity to happen. Yet in actual language use, a potentially ambiguous expression will normally be 'disambiguated' by the context in which it occurs, that is by what is said before and after. Take *Have you found the bat?* again. If it is followed by *I heard it squeaking a while ago*, the word *bat* will be taken to mean 'a flying mouse-like animal'. If it is uttered before a game of baseball, and followed by *You can borrow mine if you want* instead, then *bat* would likely mean 'a wooden club'.

Most of the time, ambiguity is unintended by the speakers or writers, who are, most likely, unaware of it. On the other hand, its purposeful, clever and effective use is often intended for humour. Groucho Marx, a famous American comedian, often used structural ambiguity to make jokes:

> *I shot an elephant in my pajamas. How he got in my pajamas, I'll never know!*

Some headlines can also be funny because they can be interpreted in more than one way:

> *7 foot doctors sue hospital*
> *More lies ahead*

Meaning connection between sentences

When sentences are put together into a text, they are not there as isolated, disconnected pieces of information. The meaning connections between them, as well as the meaning connections that hold between paragraphs, between sections, etc., are in fact what give life to a text as a coherent, organic meaningful whole.

While such meaning connections are largely implicit, to be understood in the given textual context and from certain commonly assumed perspectives, they can often be made explicit, especially in certain genres of writing like academic writing. Writers can often indicate their attitudes to what is being said or written, as well as highlight certain meaning connections over others by using a set of expressions such as *nevertheless, hence* and *especially.*

Consider *nevertheless* and *furthermore* for example. Look at how they are used to form, and accentuate, meaning linkage between sentences.

> *My father is colour-blind. Nevertheless, he is very fussy about the colour of our furniture.*
> *My father is colour-blind. Furthermore, he is tone-deaf.*

These expressions, which we will simply call 'connectives', come in various forms. Some are words, for example *therefore, besides*; some are phrases, for example *in contrast, as a result*; some can be structurally even more complex, for example *what is more, to put it differently.*

Table 2.5 gives a small sample of connectives and the different kinds of meaning connections they make.

TABLE 2.5 Connectives and their meanings

Meaning connection	Connective
Adding	*in addition, besides, moreover, furthermore* E.g. *He is one of the best poets of his generation. In addition, he is a talented painter.* *Min is always punctual. Her work, furthermore, has always been excellent.*
Emphasizing	*especially, above all, in particular, what is more* E.g. *Things have become very expensive. What is more, riding the bus now costs almost twice as much as it used to three years ago.* *I enjoyed yesterday's concert. In particular, I loved the harmonica solo.*
Restating	*in other words, put differently, that is to say* E.g. *We should let them decide for themselves. In other words, we should trust them.* *An idiom is a non-literal expression. That is to say, its meaning is different from what the words should mean.*
Comparing	*similarly, likewise, in the same way, by the same token* E.g. *Human beings need clean air. Likewise, fishes need clean water.* *Conversations bond speakers in a speech community. In the same way, writing serves to bond writers and to maintain social relationships.*
Contrasting	*but, however, nevertheless, still, yet, in contrast, in spite of, on the contrary, on the other hand* E.g. *Samantha is only 15 years old. Yet, she does more for our organization than anyone else.* *Ray is a very aggressive person. His twin brother, in contrast, is extremely shy.*
Relating to a condition	*then, in that case, under the circumstances, otherwise, if not* E.g. *She'll be spending the weekend with us. Then, you'll see how nice she is!* *We should leave now. Otherwise we will miss the flight.*
Relating to a purpose	*for this purpose, to that end, with this in mind* E.g. *Our company needs to increase productivity. To that end, the senior management have asked that we take on more roles.* *The committee must finalize the conference programme by tomorrow. For this purpose, I am calling an urgent meeting this evening.*
Stating a result	*so, therefore, thus, hence, accordingly, consequently, as a result, because, for that reason* E.g. *As a result of the accident, Jim had difficulty walking.* *The bus broke down today. Because of that, I was late for work.*

RELEVANCE TO EDUCATIONAL SETTINGS

This chapter has offered a broad overview of the structure of English. We have tried to give you a sense of what the most important concepts are, and have shared some insights into the ways in which structure conveys meaning. We have also included the basic terminology you will need in order to describe the components of English in a more specific and knowledgeable way.

Although, as teachers, we may speak English fluently, we do not automatically know how language works. For example, while you might know how to say the words *pill* and *bill* and distinguish them clearly, you will probably not know how to describe the difference in the way the two initial sounds are pronounced. Similarly, even though you are able to write grammatical sentences, and identify when a sentence is ungrammatical or ambiguous, you will probably find it very difficult to explain the reasons for the ungrammaticality or ambiguity. For example, you might know that a sentence such as *She asked me do it* is not correct, but if you do not have the **metalanguage**, that is the technical language needed to talk about language, you will probably not be able to explain the reason to learners in a way that helps them understand. It is only through the study of phonetics, morphology, syntax and semantics that you learn, as teachers, to become conscious of the way language is organized to convey meaning.

DISCUSSION AND REFLECTION QUESTIONS

1   This chapter has focused on the structure of English. Think of one other language you know – even if you don't know it well – and come up with examples for phonetics, morphology or syntax which are different from English.

2   Look at the words in italics in the sentences below. Most of these are either neologisms (new words) or words which are very rarely used. Using the morphology of these words, in particular, their suffixes, decide which word class they belong to. Give examples of similar English words in the same word classes that have the same suffixes.

    a The Greeks and the Italians are *paniverous*, unlike the Chinese and Japanese whose staple is rice.

    b The *bavardage* of the children in the playground might have irritated some, but to me it was music.

    c Stop *groaking* at my food because I'm not sharing it with you.

d The mother made sure that the food was in small *manducable* portions for her baby.

e He laughed *sclestically* like some comic-book villain!

3 The following sentences are ambiguous. Provide paraphrases for the different meanings in each case, and explain if the ambiguity is lexical or structural (or both).

a They removed the bug from his room.

b Alec paints his models standing up.

c I saw her duck.

d You can have peas and beans or carrots with the set meal.

RECOMMENDED READING AND VIEWING

Phonetics

Peter Ladefoged's book is a classic introduction to the study of phonetics.
Ladefoged, P. and Johnson, K. (2011), *A Course in Phonetics*, 6th edn. Boston, MA: Wadsworth/Cengage Learning.

The IPA's official website is worth looking at. Note that the IPA covers the speech sounds of all languages. See:
www.langsci.ucl.ac.uk/ipa/

For a very detailed glossary on phonetics, you can also look at Peter Roach's website that is linked to his phonetics textbook. See:
www.cambridge.org/other_files/cms/PeterRoach/PeterRoach_Glossary. pdf

Morphology

Harley (2006) is an introductory textbook that looks specifically at English morphology:
Harley, H. (2006), *English Words: A Linguistic Introduction*. Malden, MA: Blackwell.

English does not have a wide range of inflections. You can take a look at this website – it discusses the morphology of Greek and Latin which offer a much richer insight into the interplay between morphology and syntax. See:
www.ruf.rice.edu/~kemmer/Words/classmorph.html

Syntax

Alsagoff (2009) is an easy-to-read introduction for teachers which uses visual aids like charts and diagrams to explain English syntax, while Parrot's book is a more comprehensive book that goes into detailed discussion of syntax as well as some morphology.

Alsagoff, L. (2009), *Visual Grammar of English*, 2nd edn. Singapore: Pearson.

Parrott, M. (2000), *Grammar for English Language Teachers*. Cambridge: Cambridge University Press.

The Internet Grammar of English is a very useful website to learn about English grammar. It now also has an iOS and Android app that you can download to your mobile device! See: www.ucl.ac.uk/internet-grammar/

Semantics

Cruse (2011) is an introductory book that gives a good overview of the study of semantics as well as pragmatics.

Cruse, A. (2011), *Meaning in Language: An Introduction to Semantics and Pragmatics*. Oxford: Oxford University Press.

3

How Do We Use Language to Make Meaning?

Soe Marlar Lwin and Peter Teo

INTRODUCTION

When we see a notice *Car Sale*, as users of English, we know that it means an occasion when cars are being sold at attractive prices; but when we see a notice *Summer Sale*, we know it does not mean that summers are being sold. How is it that we interpret the two notices differently even though they look structurally similar?

As commented briefly in Chapter 1, knowing a language entails more than knowing the vocabulary and rules of grammar of the language. Our interpretation of the meaning of a piece of language is based not only on our knowledge of vocabulary and grammar rules, but also our pre-existing knowledge of the world and the environment in which the language is used. In most cases, you can understand what another language user intends to mean even when it is not explicitly stated. We saw this in the examples above. A notice *Car Sale* does not explicitly state, *We are selling cars. Do you want to buy one?*, but we can understand that intended message. In the same way, the notice *Summer Sale* does not explicitly state, *We are selling things (usually clothes) useful for summer*, but we can understand that intended message.

To be able to use a language adequately and appropriately, we learn more than the speech sounds, morphemes, word meanings and rules of putting words together to form phrases, clauses and sentences in the language (see Chapter 2). We also learn about, for example, how we use language for a purpose, how we convey that purpose to other users of the language, how we figure out the intended meaning which may not be transparent from the language form itself and so on.

This chapter introduces you to two closely related fields of Pragmatics and Discourse Analysis. Both of these fields examine language in use, and knowing more about them can help you understand how we use language to make meaning in actual situations of communication. Typically, we use a stretch of language that makes sense as a whole to communicate, rather than individual words, clauses or sentences in isolation. Therefore, studies of language in use are interested in **text** (i.e. a larger unit of linguistic structure which is above the level of clause and sentence) and **discourse** (i.e. how the purposes, participants, environments, processes, etc. of interactions play a role in the construction of texts). In this chapter, we will first look at what makes a text and how the term discourse has been explained in studies of language in use. Then we will discuss a few ways of analysing language use to understand how we use language to make meaning and how language can be used to not only express but also impose certain perspectives on the world. We will conclude the chapter with some pedagogical implications and relevance of understanding language in use to educational settings.

WHAT MAKES A TEXT?

It is not difficult for us to find examples of text. For example, we can point to a notice, a poster, a letter, a book, an email message, a short message on the mobile phone, a Facebook post, a poem, lyrics, a conversation, a lecture and the list goes on. These various examples of texts show that a text is not defined by its size or form. Some texts contain a long stretch of language (e.g. a book) while others are made up of a single sentence or even a single word (e.g. the word *Exit* above a door). What defines a text then? Also, although not all texts contain more than a single sentence, many of them do. In those texts which contain more than a single sentence, how do we make out a meaning that works across the boundaries of sentences?

To get some answers to these questions, let us compare Examples 1 and 2.

Example 1

Follow the on-screen instructions to proceed with payment. My friend drives a Volkswagen Beetle. It is planned as a country-style resort which allows people to run away from busy city life. Final preparations are also being made.

Example 2

Elephants are the biggest living land animals. There are two kinds of elephant, African and Asiatic. Both species live in herds. They have poor eyesight, but very good senses of hearing and smell. If one animal detects danger, the whole herd is alerted. (Excerpted from *Oxford Children's Encyclopedia of Our World*, 2004, p. 20.)

In Example 1, although each word has meaning and each sentence on its own makes sense, we can hardly interpret the four sentences as a meaningful unit on the whole and would find it difficult to identify as a text. On the other hand, we almost instantly recognize Example 2 as a text, are able to interpret its meaning as a unified whole and identify its purpose (e.g. to give the reader some information about elephants). A closer look at the two examples shows what distinguishes Example 2 from 1. In Example 2 there are connections or links among words as well as sentences. These connections help the reader to interpret the excerpt as a unified whole. Example 1, on the other hand, lacks these connections or links, making it a collection of unrelated sentences.

For instance, in Example 2 you can find repetition of words *elephants/ elephant*, *animals/animal*, *herds/herd*. These repetitions give us a sense of continuity of the topic as they help to maintain and reinforce the focus of the message about elephants. You can also find words and phrases which are related in meaning in Example 2. For instance, there are words which have similar meanings like *kinds* and *species*. They are called **synonyms**. Like repetition, synonyms help to maintain the continuity of the topic across sentences by reiterating the same items or events. However, unlike repetition, synonyms help to add variety and avoid monotony which can be caused by overusing the same words or phrases.

In Example 2, you might also notice that words like *eyesight*, *hearing* and *smell* are related – they are different types of senses. We call 'type of' word relationship hyponymy. *Eyesight*, *hearing* and *smell* are **hyponyms** of the word *senses*. In fact, the words *eyesight*, *hearing* and *smell* are also related to the word *elephant* – these senses are part of an elephant. We call 'part of' word relationship meronymy. So, *eyesight*, *hearing* and *smell* are also **meronyms** of *elephant*. Hyponyms and meronyms help to establish links within or across sentences because they help the reader to create a network of keywords or concepts through an awareness of the relationships among words and phrases used in different parts of a text.

Besides the links created through the use of repeated or related words and phrases, there are also certain grammatical features which help to establish links among sentences in Example 2. For instance, the **pronoun** *they* in the fourth sentence refers back to the noun *elephants* in the first sentence. Links are made between these two sentences as the reader must interpret what *they* in the fourth sentence means by referring back to the first sentence. A similar grammatical feature that helps to create links by making the reader refer to what is stated in the earlier or later parts of a sentence is called **ellipsis** (i.e. omission of certain element in a structure). In Example 2, after saying there are two kinds of elephants, the two types are given – *African and Asiatic*. Notice that there is no need to say *African elephant* or *Asiatic elephant*. Ellipsis makes you refer back to what has been stated earlier in the sentence. **Conjunction** is another grammatical feature which helps to create links. In Example 2, *but* signals that what is to follow has an opposing relationship with what went before by conceding other types of senses (besides the eyesight) that an elephant has.

In linguistics, we use the term **cohesion** to refer to the connections or links that exit in a stretch of language and that help to identify it as a text. The language features that help to establish such links are called cohesive devices. Specifically, we call the links created through the repetition of words or the use of words which are related in meanings (such as synonyms and hyponyms as in the above examples) **lexical cohesion**. Links established through the use of grammatical features (such as pronoun, ellipsis and conjunction) are referred to as **grammatical cohesion**.

A comprehensive study on cohesion was done by M. A. K. Halliday and R. Hasan, which was published in 1976. Their study is still considered a classic work in this area. Halliday and Hasan explain that cohesive relationships occur when we depend on or presuppose the interpretation of another element to interpret some element in a set of sentences. They also explain that such cohesive relationships within and between the sentences help us to identify the set of sentences as a text. Subsequent studies of text and discourse have explained in detail different types of cohesive devices (e.g. see Carter et al., 2008).

Cohesion is crucial in making judgement on whether the stretch of language can be identified as a text. However, the internal textual connections created through the use of various cohesive devices would not be sufficient to explain how a text is formed. Consider Example 3 below.

Example 3

Follow the on-screen instructions to proceed with payment. Payment is made in dollars every month. The last month of a year is December. It is the coldest period of the year, and May the warmest. Therefore, we decided to travel then.

You will be able to identify several links among words and sentences in Example 3, such as:

- repetition of words *payment*, *month*, *year*;
- the use of words which are related in meaning, for example,
  ○ December and May are part of a year – that is, the words *December* and *May* are meronyms of the word *year*,
  ○ *coldest* and *warmest* are words with opposite meanings or **antonyms**;
- the pronoun *it* refers back to the word *December*;
- the conjunction *therefore* indicates a causal connection and so on.

Although the set of sentences in Example 3 is highly cohesive, it is still hard for us to interpret these sentences as a unified whole and to figure out the purpose or situation in or for which this stretch of language is produced.

Example 3 shows that cohesion alone is not sufficient to ensure that a piece of language makes sense and to identify it as a text. As a reader, you must be able to make other meaningful connections which are not expressed by words and sentences but which are achieved by relating the piece of language to the context, for example to the purpose and audience for which it is produced, the situation in which it is produced and the experience and knowledge about people and the world. In Example 3, you find it difficult to make such a connection to the context and to arrive at an interpretation of its purpose. This kind of connection which can be achieved only by relating the piece of language to the context is called **coherence**.

In summary, to make sense of a stretch of language that contains more than a single word or sentence and to call it a text, we do not merely rely on cohesion or the internal links created through language devices. We must also be able to make other meaningful connections, for example to the purpose, audience, situation and so on to establish coherence. For those examples which contain only a single word (like the word *Exit*), it is when we can relate it to the context such as the situation (above a door) and the purpose (to give direction), that we recognize it as a text.

TEXT AND DISCOURSE

Understanding cohesion and coherence as the two properties of a text helps us realize the close relationship between language and context. In general, context refers to the environment or circumstances surrounding the way in which we use language. However, for an understanding of how communication and meaning-making occur through the interaction between language and context, we need to acknowledge that context is multifaceted. It involves several aspects, such as the immediate situation (e.g. the physical setting where the language is used, the purpose, the people who are involved, etc.) as well as the wider sociocultural context (e.g. what we know about certain social occasions, cultural ceremonies and beliefs, visions and missions of a particular institution, etc.).

The two aspects of situational and sociocultural context are sometimes referred to as the 'non-linguistic context' in order to distinguish them from the 'linguistic context'. The linguistic context means the words, phrases, clauses or sentences that co-occur with the particular word, phrase, clause or sentence under consideration. For example, the linguistic context of the word *co-occur* in the preceding sentence will be all the words and phrases that come before or after it. Often the linguistic context is more appropriately referred to as 'co-text' or the surrounding text.

In the studies of language in use, the term 'discourse' (instead of 'text') is often used to emphasize that the focus of inquiry in such studies is the relationship or interaction between text *and* context (rather than limiting the investigation to only the analysis of features found within a text). Some linguists use the two terms almost interchangeably to refer to a unit of language above the level of clause and sentence (e.g. see Carter et al., 2008). Others such as H. G. Widdowson (2007) define text as the (physical) product and discourse as the process of text production which includes the motivations behind its production and the interpretation by readers or hearers. Rising above the problems with the two terms, a common concern among those who study language in use is to look at language as it is produced and interpreted in and for actual situations of communication. With a plethora of texts around us, we should look at how texts can be classified before we discuss ways of analysing language use.

CLASSIFICATION OF TEXTS

We can categorize texts found commonly around us in many different ways. Two possible ways are (a) based on the mode or channel of communication in which a text is produced and (b) based on their different social purposes. We will first look at classification of texts according to the mode of communication. Classification of texts according to their different social purposes will be discussed in connection with ways of analysing language use in the later section.

By and large, spoken and written communication could be considered two 'primary' systems or modes of communication involving the use of language. Thus one way of categorizing texts is to make a distinction between 'spoken' and 'written' texts. However, such a distinction should be used only as starting points to help us explore the complexities of language use, rather than as 'pure' binary categories. Treating spoken and written texts as binary categories would only lead to more confusion than clarity, as will be seen when we look at the characteristics of different types of texts.

Spoken and written texts

Spoken language is transient, unless it is recorded. One characteristic of spoken texts is that they are typically produced spontaneously for current listeners, for example a conversation that you have with your friends during lunch. In the process of a conversation, each participant chips in with comments, feedback, questions, clarification, etc. All of these help to shape the conversation. On the other hand, in producing a written text (e.g. a chapter in a textbook), the writer is typically separated in time and/or space from the reader. A good example is the lapse between the time we are writing this chapter and the time you will be reading it. Interpretation of the writer's intention by the reader is therefore displaced and delayed. Written texts are typically planned, edited and permanent, as compared with spoken texts (see also Chapter 6).

The two examples of spoken and written texts, a conversation with friends and a chapter in a textbook, should be viewed as a kind of continuum. You can think of various other types of spoken and written texts which we produce and interpret in our daily life and which lie somewhere along the continuum. For example, spoken texts such as interviews, announcements, news broadcasts, storytelling and political speeches are produced with different degrees of planning for the speaker and different kinds of listener involvement. Such differences in the degree of planning and listener involvement can result in varying amounts of overlaps, pauses, false starts and other **non-fluency features** like fillers (e.g. *er, umm*) in different types of spoken texts. We typically find many of these features in a spontaneous conversation. However, news broadcasts and scripted speech, although they are produced in the spoken mode, are planned and rehearsed. So, it is less likely that you will find non-fluency features in news broadcasts and scripted speech. Similarly, you can think of examples of written texts which are produced with little planning and which show 'speech-like' features such as incomplete sentences (i.e. with the Subject or Verb omitted). A note we scribble and leave for a colleague just before we rush to our class: *Gotta go teach! Will pop by later* is an example of this type of written texts.

It is also important to note that when we communicate, either in the spoken or written mode, the language we use is typically accompanied by other features. For example, when we talk, our **utterances** are typically accompanied by features such as gestures and facial expressions, which convey meaning through a different mode of communication (i.e. the visual mode). Similarly, most of our written texts contain different typefaces (e.g. bold, italics, capitals) to foreground a certain meaning. Very often, written texts are also accompanied by images (e.g. diagrams, pictures) that convey a certain meaning through the visual mode. Therefore, texts we produce and interpret are usually **multimodal** (i.e. more than one mode of communication is used in a single text, and meanings are constructed through interaction between features from different modes). For studies of language in use, a multimodal analysis of texts examines not only how language conveys meaning as an individual mode but also how it interacts with features from other mode(s) to create possibilities for more profound interpretation of texts.

New-media texts

With the advancement of new communication technologies, communication nowadays is more and more computer-mediated (e.g. email, SMS, blogs, discussion boards, Facebook, Twitter, etc.). We usually call those texts which are produced in computer-mediated communication new-media texts. New-media texts have posed a challenge to the notion of a purely spoken or written text. They show certain characteristics which are similar to a spoken interaction (e.g. features related to the simultaneous nature of interaction between the two users, such as turn-taking and non-fluency features). At the same time, they also use resources from the written mode (e.g. spelling and punctuation). Thus, a defining characteristic of new-media texts is their hybrid nature. Crystal (2001; 2006) uses the term 'Netspeak' to refer to the language used in this new medium of linguistic communication. Studies interested in this type of texts often investigate how technology affects the way we use language.

Importance of social purpose

It must be stressed that technology or the mode of communication is not the only factor which affects the way we use language. The social relationship between language users and the purpose are as important as the mode in which language is used. For example, it is very likely that in your email/SMS inbox, you can find considerable variation of language features used in the messages sent by different people. Texts, whether they are spoken, written, multimodal or produced in new media, can be further categorized according to their different social purposes. The mode in which a text is produced interacts with various aspects of the context in which it is produced. In the following section, we will discuss a few ways of analysing language to find out some key principles and patterns of spoken and written language in use.

ANALYSING LANGUAGE USE

Our examples for cohesion and coherence in the earlier section focus on samples of written language. Although in general the principles of cohesion and coherence also apply to spoken language, the ways we create connections to interpret meanings when we are engaged in a spoken interaction can be more subtle. Let us examine Example 4, a brief example of conversation or a type of spoken text most familiar to language users.

Example 4

Jane: I've got two movie tickets for tonight.

Betty: I need to hand in my assignment by 8 am tomorrow.

Jane: Ok, I'll go and ask Susie.

Apart from the words *tonight* and *tomorrow*, which suggest a temporal sequence, there are very few obvious links between the above utterances, and the whole conversational exchange seems incoherent. How does each speaker in Example 4 make sense of what the other says? In fact, like the two speakers, you will probably have no difficulty to arrive at an interpretation that Betty has declined Jane's invitation to go to the movie, which is not actually expressed by the words. We arrive at such interpretations by drawing **inferences** based on our knowledge of the world and how such a conversational exchange works, for example,

- when someone has movie tickets for two, she will invite someone else to go with her, so we would interpret Jane's first utterance as an invitation to Betty;

- Betty's utterance follows Jane's invitation, so we interpret it as Betty's response to Jane's invitation;

- when someone is trying to finish an assignment urgently, she has no time to do other things such as going to a movie, so we interpret Betty's response (as Jane does) as a rejection of Jane's invitation.

We do not, of course, consciously work through such processes of making connections and drawing conclusions while we are engaged in a conversation. However, thinking about how we make sense of a seemingly incoherent conversational exchange in this way helps us to understand how speakers imply meaning and how hearers draw inferences to interpret speakers' intention. Hearers use not only the meanings of the words but also some knowledge of the context to interpret speakers' intention or implied meaning. The field of study which examines those aspects of meaning which depend more on the context and the speaker's intention than the meanings of the actual words in an utterance is known as Pragmatics.

Generally speaking, Pragmatics focuses on how we communicate through language in spoken contexts. However, pragmatic principles can also be relevant to the ways we use and interpret meanings in written context. Historically, theoretical perspectives of pragmatics are informed not only by linguistics but also by philosophy. A philosopher of language, Paul Grice, proposed that there are a number of principles governing the way we communicate through utterances in context. When we are engaged in a conversation, we tacitly subscribe to these principles. We will now look at some of these principles.

Cooperative principles

Grice (1975) calls the principles governing the way we communicate through utterances the 'cooperative principles' and describes them in terms of four maxims:

- The maxim of quantity: (Be brief) Make your contribution as informative as is required, do not make it more or less informative than is required.

- The maxim of quality: (Be true) Do not say what you believe to be false or for which you lack adequate evidence.

- The maxim of relation: (Be relevant) Make your contribution relevant.

- The maxim of manner: (Be clear) Avoid ambiguity and be orderly.

Much of our day-to-day conversation follows these maxims. For example,

Guest: Where's the executive seminar room?

Receptionist: It's in admin building, level two.

Here, the receptionist has provided the right amount of information (quantity) and has truthfully (quality), directly (relation) and clearly (manner) answered the question. Speakers often use some expressions to show that they are aware of these maxims. For example, *to cut a long story short* (quantity), *as far as I know* (quality), *by the way* (relation), *I'm not sure if this makes sense* (manner).

According to Grice, conversation should work without problem if speakers followed the maxims. However, as we all know, we often encounter conversations in which speakers flout the cooperative principles – that is, they (purposely) do not observe the maxims. In fact, it may be socially acceptable (and perhaps even preferred), to flout certain maxims for reasons of politeness. For example, when your friend asks you if you like his or her new haircut, you don't and you reply: *Oh, I know that hair salon, it has very modern interior design and I saw their ads very recently in the paper.* Your reply flouts the maxims of quantity, quality and manner as it does not truthfully and clearly provide the right amount of information (i.e. yes/no) to the question. By flouting the maxims, you hope your friend interprets your answer as *No, I don't*, without feeling offended.

Thinking about spoken texts in terms of the cooperative principles can help us uncover the underlying assumptions made by speakers and the inferences hearers have to make. However, we should be careful not to assume that these maxims and cooperative principles are universal. Preferred ways of managing successful cooperative communication can differ from language to language. In a culture where clarity and directness are associated with politeness, speakers will likely follow the maxims of quantity, quality, relation and manner as proposed by Grice. However, if a culture views indirectness as most polite and more appropriate, speakers will follow different principles such as evading brief, true, direct and clear utterances to achieve successful communication. We will look at some examples of culture-specific preferences in our discussion of direct and indirect speech acts below.

Speech acts

Another important aspect of language use is how language users choose a particular form of language so that it will be considered appropriate (i.e. it will fall within the expectations of other users of the language). When we use language, we not only produce meaningful utterances or sentences, we also do different things or perform different actions through language, which are known as **speech acts**. Philosophers of language, such as John Austin and John Searle, proposed a theory on speech acts which states that producing a meaningful utterance is more than producing a meaningful linguistic expression (Searle, 1992). Some of the speech acts we often use can perform an action. For example, by saying *I apologize*, I have made an apology; by saying *I promise*, I have made a promise to someone. Of course, certain utterances need to be said by the right person under the right circumstances to perform the action. For example, *I declare open a Convocation for the presentation of graduates of the degree of Bachelor of Education*, needs to be said by the chancellor or the pro-chancellor of the university to perform the opening of the convocation ceremony.

Apart from these 'performative' utterances, there are in fact many other actions that all of us do through language. Perhaps the three most common speech acts we use daily are informing (i.e. giving information), questioning (i.e. asking for information) and requesting or commanding (i.e. getting someone to do something). We do these actions directly or indirectly. For example, in English, if we want someone to read a chapter, we can say:

(i) It would be good if you could read this chapter.

(ii) Would you mind reading this chapter?

(iii) Read this chapter.

Different languages will have different word order or 'rules' of placing the Subject, Verb, Object, etc. to form a sentence or utterance that is used for informing, questioning and requesting or commanding. In English, the declarative form (Subject > Verb . . .) is characteristically associated with informing. The interrogative form (Finite > Subject > rest of Verb . . .) is characteristically associated with questioning and the imperative form (Verb . . .) with requesting or commanding someone to do something.

In the examples of requesting someone to read the chapter, the first example uses the declarative form and the second uses the interrogative form. We regard these two examples as indirect speech acts of requesting in English because they use a form or construction other than the characteristic imperative form to request someone to do something. Only the third example uses the characteristic imperative form, which is regarded as a direct speech act of requesting in English. Just as the same function (e.g. requesting someone to do something) can be achieved through the use of different forms (i.e. imperative, interrogative or declarative), the same form can serve different functions. For example, the interrogative form, *Can you move your leg?*, functions as a question for a doctor who is trying to get some information for a diagnosis of a patient's injury. The same form serves as a request when it is used because you want someone's leg which is blocking your way to be moved.

The examples of requesting someone to read the chapter might suggest that indirect speech acts appear to be more polite in English. However, it is important to note that, depending on the context (e.g. who the speaker and the hearer are), the use of indirectness can be for other meanings (e.g. sarcasm, threat, display of frustration, etc.) than politeness. You can think of a situation when the mother uses an indirect form, *Would you mind picking up your dirty clothes on the floor?*, to her son. Also, the relationship between indirectness and politeness can be different across cultures. For example, speakers of English and German conventionally perceive indirect speech acts as more polite and use them more frequently in making requests, whereas speakers of Polish and Russian use direct requests most frequently as they tend to associate directness with honesty and politeness (Ogiermann, 2009). Chinese speakers in China are also said to prefer using direct request forms (Lee-Wong, 1994).

Specific features of language to display politeness can be different from language to language. For example, English speakers might use syntactic means such as the interrogative sentence construction to display indirectness and politeness when making a request. In Myanmar (Burmese), addition of lexical words such as diminutives (e.g. *small, a little*), rather than the sentence construction, helps to display less imposition on the listener and thus is considered more polite. Below are examples of i. a request and ii. a polite request to open the door in Myanmar:

i တံခါး ဖွင့် ပါ။

   Door open verb particle for request.

ii တံခါး လေး တဆိတ်လောက် ဖွင့် ပါ။

   Door small a little open verb particle for request.

Other features of language used in different languages as the main politeness devices include address terms (e.g. in Vietnamese) and honorifics with morphological variations (e.g. in Korean).

These cross-cultural examples show different ways of displaying politeness in different languages. Users of a particular language decide when to use these features depending on the social context (e.g. who they are speaking or writing to and for what purposes). Next, we will discuss how we choose particular language forms depending on the social context.

Register

Studies have used a 'functional approach' to discourse analysis to find out how the ways we use language are closely related to different social contexts. Fundamentally, a functional approach relates the choices of particular language features used in a text to the three specific factors constituting the **register** or immediate context of situation. The three factors are outlined in Figure 3.1.

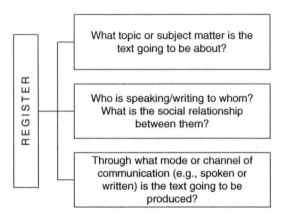

FIGURE 3.1 *Register and its constituents*

As an example, we can compare a written text of legal matters printed on the back of an airline ticket and addressed to all passengers in general, and a conversation between two close friends about their lost baggage.

- legal writing
Liability for loss, delay or damage to baggage is limited unless a higher value is declared in advance and additional charges are paid. (Excerpted from *IATA Conditions of Contract and Other Important Notices*)

- conversation between friends
A: I told you, don't leave your b(ag)
B: No but I thought you'd keep an eye on it . . . well . . . erm
A: Ok let's go and ask the airline staff.

Differences between the two texts in terms of register can be outlined as in Table 3.1.

TABLE 3.1 Legal writing versus conversation

Register	Legal writing	Conversation
Subject matter	Conditions of liability for various baggage mishaps	Blame for someone's lost baggage
Social relationship	Far and distant – addressees are not individually or personally identified	Close and personal
Mode of communication	Written – carefully planned	Spoken – spontaneous

You will find that different language features are used in the two examples depending on the subject matter, the social relationship between the language users and the mode of communication through which the respective text was produced. In a written text of legal matters printed on the back of an airline ticket and addressed to all passengers in general, you will find the use of formal vocabulary (e.g. *declared*) and legal jargon (e.g. *liability*) as well as complex and complete sentences, but no personal pronouns. In contrast, a conversation between two close friends about their lost baggage contains several uses of personal pronouns *I*, *you*, informal vocabulary (e.g. *keep an eye on*), as well as interruption and non-fluency features, which are characteristics of a spontaneous conversation.

Genres

In a broader sense, a functional approach holds the view that the wider sociocultural context, such as the distinctive purposes of producing texts in society, is what shapes its overall structure as well as choices of vocabulary and grammatical patterns. Based on this view, texts can be categorized according to their different social purposes. The term **genres** is used to refer to ways of achieving distinct social purposes through the use of particular language forms. A genre analysis is usually done to highlight the typical structural components and language features characterizing particular text types such as:

- Narrative (e.g. folktales),
- Recount (e.g. retelling of what one did during a visit to the zoo),
- Instruction (e.g. manual to assemble a piece of furniture),

- Information report (e.g. encyclopaedia entry on elephants),

- Explanation (e.g. about water cycle),

- Discussion and argument (e.g. essay on why smoking on campus should be banned).

Each of these text types serves distinct purposes within society. For example, one of the social purposes of narrative is to entertain hearers or readers by appealing to their imagination. To achieve this purpose, a narrative text typically has the following structural components.

- Orientation: Introducing the main characters, when and where the events took place.

- Complication: The main action or salient events leading to a conflict or unexpected/unusual occurrence.

- Resolution: What happened in the end.

A series of events and a problem (e.g. some unexpected or unusual element) are put together through these structural components in a narrative.

In addition to these overall structural components, a narrative text will contain certain language features such as nouns that identify the characters as specific participants (e.g. *John, Ah Mei, Goldilocks*) and verbs in past tense to state fictitious or factual events that have happened. Just as there are different ways of displaying politeness, features which are considered to be crucial to make a narrative good or bad can be culture and language specific. For example, relating a series of events in chronological order is considered necessary but not sufficient in English narratives. English speakers would expect evaluative comments which convey the storyteller's attitudes about events and their interpretations of characters' motives and reactions. However, in Japanese, less emphasis is given on evaluative descriptions since omitting the teller's emotion or telling without verbalizing the teller's feelings is preferred (Minami, 2008).

Understanding text types is helpful for us to explain (and teach) how language is used for different social purposes. However, in the real world, there are very few 'pure' texts as such. Most texts are hybrid, that is features of more than one text type are combined in a single text, to serve a range of different social purposes. Moreover, language users often deliberately manipulate the features typical of a text type to achieve certain effects or for a particular purpose. For example, in order to entice the reader to read on, a text about a recipe can begin with a personal recount of the authors preparing and enjoying the meal before giving the instructions on how to make these dishes (e.g. see Lake Breakfast www.sailingbreezes.com/Sailing_Breezes_Current/Other_Reviews/feasts_afloat.htm).

Analysing language use can help us to investigate further possible intentions or purposes of text production, target audience and certain interpretations which may otherwise be unnoticed. In the next section, we will look at how language can be used to not only express but also impose certain perspectives on the world.

LANGUAGE AND POWER

In his book called *Language and Power* published in 1989, Norman Fairclough put forth a cogent argument of how language is not merely a neutral and objective communicative tool that reflects the 'reality' in society but is instrumental in reproducing power relations in society. In addition to being a tool to communicate information and express emotions or intentions, language can also be a means to exert power over people. Critical Discourse Analysis, or CDA as it is more popularly known, is a branch of discourse analysis dedicated to exploring the relationship between language and power. Basically, people who 'do' CDA are interested in answering the question: How does language express and reinforce power relations between people? In what follows, we discuss with reference to a few examples how language exerts, shapes and perpetuates power.

When a news reporter interviews and quotes people in positions of power, such as politicians, CEOs, university professors and police chiefs (regardless of whether they are male or female), the reporter is in fact presenting a biased view of the news events and of the world in general. Newspapers have a tendency to quote from authoritative sources in an attempt to make their reports seem credible and reliable. However, this tendency to quote people who are already in positions of power and authority – both directly and indirectly – results in a predominantly establishment view of the world, where ordinary people are only entitled to their experiences but not their opinions. In this way, the use of quotation becomes a gatekeeping device that admits those in positions of power and influence while shutting out the opinions and perspectives of those deemed powerless by society. Thus, while the powerful become more powerful through quotation patterns that enhance their status and visibility, the systematic silencing of the powerless – the poor, the young, the uneducated, the unemployed, the elderly, etc. – only further disempowers them. It is this partial and biased view of the world that newspapers tend to reproduce which has led scholars like Roger Fowler to comment: 'The world of the Press is not the real world, but a world skewed and judged' (1991, p. 11).

As a concrete example of how the press tends to distort and interpret news events for its readers, let us refer to a couple of texts which appeared in the *YahooNews* website following the disaster caused by Hurricane Katrina which devastated parts of New Orleans in the USA in 2005. Due to copyright restrictions, only the descriptions of the photographs accompanying the text excerpts are given. Readers can view the photographs at http://rawstory. com/news/2005/Blogs_raise_questions_of_racism_in_hurricane_photo_ cap_0902.html

Text 1
Two residents wade through chest-deep water after finding bread and soda from a local grocery store after Hurricane Katrina came through the area in New Orleans, Louisiana.
Accompanying Text 1 is a photograph showing a woman and a man carrying backpacks walking in water that is about chest deep. The woman is holding what appears to be a carton of soft drinks. The woman and man appear to be Caucasian based on their light skin colour.

Text 2
A young man walks through chest deep flood water after looting a grocery store in New Orleans on Tuesday, Aug 30, 2005. Flood waters continue to rise in New Orleans after Hurricane Katrina did extensive damage . . .
Accompanying Text 2 is a photograph of a boy walking in chest-deep water with one hand holding what appears to be a large trash bag whose contents are not visible and another hand cradling what looks like a carton of milk. The dark-skinned boy appears to be of Hispanic origin.

Texts 1 and 2 represent two very similar news reports on the same event, but with two very different messages. The first depicts the Caucasian-looking couple as resourceful even courageous, being able to 'find' food in times of crisis, whereas the second portrays the youth, possibly of Hispanic origin, as a lawless vagrant who 'loots' and preys on others in times of crisis. Moreover, we are told that the couple in Text 1 are 'residents', which seems to legitimize their presence, whereas in Text 2 the boy is described merely as 'a young man', which seems to ascribe to him more maturity (and hence greater culpability) than what the photograph suggests. If a picture paints a thousand words (because 'seeing is believing'), then the pictures combine with the words in the reports to convey a powerful message: One race is portrayed as resourceful while another is depicted to be stooping to crime. From this example, we can see how visual and language resources interact in a multimodal text to present a world that is 'skewed and judged'. In this way, we witness the power that texts like newspaper reports wield to reinforce and even perpetuate racist beliefs that might harbour in the minds of people.

Issues to do with the relationship between language and power are not only to be found in newspapers or the mass media. In fact, they can be found everywhere, including classrooms. Being an expert adult, the teacher is someone who exerts power and authority over the students. This is done in the way the teacher controls who gets to speak about what in class. What counts as 'relevant' and 'valued' in what students say or write about in class, who can speak when, what questions students can/should ask in class, whether they can challenge the contents of their textbooks or even the teacher's notes and so on are all determined unilaterally by the teacher, and these are just some of the more common means by which the teacher in a classroom exerts control and power over students. Power as it is transmitted and reinforced through language is therefore a much more pervasive phenomenon in society than what most people think.

RELEVANCE TO EDUCATIONAL SETTINGS

Through our discussion of how language is used to make meaning in actual situations of communication, we have shown that in learning a language you must also learn how to interpret and produce cohesive and coherent stretches of language. You also learn how to choose the vocabulary and grammatical patterns appropriate for your intended audience and purposes. An awareness of how language is used differently in different contexts (such as at home with family members and in schools with teachers and peers) and how language is instrumental in reproducing power relations in society or institution (including schools) is helpful for you to understand why children have to learn a new set of 'rules' of language use when they enter schools. For example, a child has to learn to bid for a turn by raising her hand to talk during a lesson. It opens up another area of inquiry that examines discourse features of classroom interaction and texts used and produced in classrooms. These are discussed further in Chapter 7.

An understanding of cultural differences in the principles and patterns of language use can also help teachers to avoid mistakenly judging a child from a different cultural background as socially, academically or intellectually deficient when the child's use of language mismatches the principles and patterns expected at schools. Minami (2008) gave an example of a Japanese boy who told a story with little verbalization of his feelings – a preferred way of storytelling in the Japanese culture – but was misinterpreted by his American teacher as lacking imagination and creativity. Knowledge of culturally preferred patterns of language use also serves as a basis for teachers to reflect on such issues as identity, attitudes, values and power surrounding cross-cultural (mis) communication in a multicultural society or a multicultural situation which is common in many classrooms today.

DISCUSSION AND REFLECTION QUESTIONS

1 **a** What kind of speech act (e.g. apologizing, questioning, informing, etc.) is performed by the following notice found on a public toilet door?

THANK YOU FOR KEEPING THE TOILET CLEAN AND DRY.

b Can you think of other language forms or sentence constructions which can be used to achieve a similar function as the above notice? For each of the construction you can think of, explain whether it performs a direct or indirect speech act.

2 **a** Identify different types of lexical and grammatical cohesion found in the following text, and briefly explain how they work as cohesive devices.

Trust that your wisdom and good judgment will bring relief early in the month. Although some of your idealism has to be sacrificed, the facts you face now will help you make more appropriate plans for achieving your lofty goals. After the 14th, be patient with family. Real estate moves may be temporarily delayed, but an exciting domestic shift remains in store for you. (Excerpted from *BAZAAR*, Feb. 2007)

b Giving examples of specific language features, discuss what you think are the purpose(s) and the kind of social relationship between the writer and the reader.

3 The following is an extract from a news report about riots in the English city of Bristol which appeared in Singapore's mainstream newspaper, *The Straits Times*:

Riots erupted on Thursday night after two men were killed when the stolen police motorcycle they were riding was involved in a crash with an unmarked police car.

Comment on how the 'reality' changes when the same news event is reported in the following ways, and the possible motivations behind them:

a Two men died after the stolen police motorcycle they were riding collided with an unmarked police car.

b Police killed two 17-year-olds on a motorcycle by crashing their unmarked police car into them.

c Two youths killed themselves by crashing their stolen motorcycle into a police car.

RECOMMENDED READING AND VIEWING

For very readable explanations and discussions of key concepts in discourse analysis, see:

Widdowson, H. G. (2007), *Discourse Analysis*. Oxford: Oxford University Press.

For wide-ranging yet accessible information about linguistic tools for analysis of a variety of texts (with many activities and examples), see:

Carter, R., Goddard, A., Reah, D., Sanger, K. and Swift, N. (2008), *Working with Texts: A Core Introduction to Language Analysis* (3rd edn). London and New York, NY: Routledge.

For a comprehensive introduction to key pragmatic principles, see:

Cutting, J. (2002), *Pragmatics and Discourse: A Resource Book for Students*. London and New York, NY: Routledge.

For an example of a text (*Lake Breakfast*) which combines two text types, see:

www.sailingbreezes.com/Sailing_Breezes_Current/Other_Reviews/feasts_afloat.htm

For the two photographs accompanying the two news reports on Hurricane Katrina, see:

http://rawstory.com/news/2005/Blogs_raise_questions_of_racism_in_hurricane_photo_cap_0902.html

4

Why Is There Variation within a Language?

Anthea Fraser Gupta

INTRODUCTION

It would be a dull world in which everyone looked alike, dressed alike, always ate the same food – or spoke alike. There is variation in language, as in every other aspect of human behaviour, because people vary. The differences in the way different people use language follow patterns that are motivated by our human need to be both an individual and a group member. We use language to express both our individuality and our belongingness.

There are many languages in the world, and within every language there is variation. **Linguistic variation**, quite simply, refers to the range of different ways of using the same language. There isn't just one way of speaking or writing a language. Some aspects of the pronunciation, spelling, grammar and vocabulary of a language vary depending on a range of things. All languages have variation, but most of my examples will come from English, as it is the only language that I can be sure my readers know.

There are many kinds of linguistic variation, generally divided in two kinds: (a) variation by what you are doing and (b) variation by who you are. We have seen in Chapter 3 how languages are used differently depending on what a speaker is doing. There is a great deal of variation in English associated with variation in text type. For example, no one uses the same **style** to write a recipe as to chat about cooking with a friend. In this chapter, I will explain linguistic variation by who you are, in terms of your regional origins and your other social characteristics. Chapter 3 discussed some of the ways in which social meaning is conveyed, as well as how linguistic structures differ depending on text type. The two types of variation (what you do and who you are) are connected, but it is often easier to understand what is going on if we try to keep them apart to some extent.

REGIONAL VARIATION

Linguistic variation has been studied in various ways over the centuries. The most obvious kind of linguistic variation is variation in speech depending on where speakers come from. For example, English speakers who have spent all their lives in New York will speak differently from those who have spent all their lives in Sydney. Most languages are spoken over wide enough areas to show this **regional variation**. The longer a language has been spoken in the same place, the more regional variation there will be in the way that it is spoken. For example, in England, where English has been spoken for about 1,500 years, there can be noticeable differences in the speech of people from settlements just 20 kms from each other, while in Australia, where English has been spoken for just over 200 years, regional differences are much smaller, despite the much greater area of Australia. Regional variation develops partly because places that are geographically apart develop differently and partly because people develop group identities: We want to be members of a group, so we behave like the people we mix with. Most of us want people to know where we are from. If we want people to believe we are from somewhere else, we will probably have to adopt a different way of speaking.

In all languages, there are differences in terms of the way in which people pronounce the speech sounds of the same language. In English, for example, the way people say the vowels of *horse, dog,* and *cat* might give you some information about where they come from. There are a number of different ways in which these vowels can be pronounced. Such pronunciation differences are large in languages such as English, Spanish and Arabic, which are spoken over wide areas. We can say that speakers who use different speech sounds have different **accents**. Variation in the pronunciation of speech sounds is the main area of focus in studies of linguistic variation, but cannot be studied without a good knowledge of phonetics. If you want to understand more about phonetics, I recommend Ladefoged's book (2006): The online version of it allows you to hear what sounds the phonetic symbols represent. For this chapter, I will give examples that do not expect a knowledge of phonetics (see Chapter 2). Phonetic symbols are those in square brackets (like [d]); slash lines (like /d/) are used for **phonemes**, which are speech sounds in a specific language or dialect. When I use a phonetic symbol without an explanation, you can assume that the sound is the normal one represented by the letter in the writing of English.

You will be aware of many regional differences in accent, both in English and in any other languages known to you. Most of these concern quite subtle differences in the pronunciation of vowels. There are also differences in the pronunciation of consonants. For example, in many languages, there is regional variation in the sound associated with the letter 'r'. I will represent this speech sound by /r/. The way a /r/ is formed varies from one place to another in many languages (including English, German, French, Malay, Italian, Mandarin Chinese). For example, the sound /r/ might be trilled on the tongue. In the International Phonetic Alphabet (IPA), this is represented by the symbol [r]. Or it might be produced by sending a smooth stream of air across a tongue raised up at the ridge behind the upper teeth: This is represented in the IPA by [ɹ]. If you go to Ladefoged's clickable IPA chart and click on [r] and [ɹ] (and on the other symbols that look something like an 'r') you will hear the differences in the way a /r/ speech sound can be pronounced.

In English (and in some other languages, including Mandarin Chinese and German), there are also important regional differences in the context in which a /r/ is pronounced. In some accents of English (such as most accents from the USA, Scotland, Ireland and the Philippines), a /r/ is usually or always pronounced in every word in which it is present in the spelling. For speakers of those accents, there is a /r/ in *run, merry, far,* and *farm.* But other speakers (including most people from England, Australia, South Africa and India) pronounce a /r/ only when it is followed by a vowel. In these accents, there would be a /r/ in *run* and *merry,* but no /r/ in *far* or *farm.* This important difference in accent has consequences for the way in which vowels are pronounced in English, as accents in which the /r/ has been lost have developed several different vowels in order to make distinctions between words like *bee* and *beer,* or *cot* and *court.* Accents that do not pronounce the /r/ in all positions also have more words that sound alike: In those accents *paw* and *pour* are likely to sound exactly the same. In words in which there is a letter 'r' at the end of a word, speakers who do not pronounce a final /r/ might pronounce /r/ when a vowel follows (as in *pour out,* or *pouring*), but many speakers of these accents, unless they are speaking very carefully, and remembering the spelling, will also put a /r/ in the middle of *pawing,* which sounds odd to speakers who pronounce a final /r/ in *pour* but not in *paw.* The regional variation that is linked to the distribution of /r/ in English creates a particular difficulty in the teaching of English pronunciation to second language learners, especially at the early stages of learning, when it is a good idea to teach a single accent.

Regional variation is not just in pronunciation. English users are likely to know that there are some differences in the words used for the same thing in different regions. For example, in different regions of the world, the back part of a car is called either the *trunk*, the *boot* or the *dicky*. There is also regional variation in grammar: For example in some regions, the past tense of the verb DIVE is *dived* and in others it is *dove*.

For this discussion, a **dialect** is a subdivision of a language depending on region. The term 'dialect' is used differently by different writers. Some use it to refer to linguistic variation based on any social features (especially region, social class and gender). Others use it to refer only to regional differences in accent, grammar or vocabulary. Others use it to refer only to regional varieties that have differences in grammar and vocabulary as well as in accent. Some use dialect to mean 'non-standard dialect'. You need to be aware of the differences in definition when reading about dialects.

Some of the oldest surviving written texts comment on differences in the way people from one region speak compared to people from other regions. Philosophers and creative writers have long had an interest in identifying and explaining the ways in which people from different regions speak the same language. Two thousand years ago, the Chinese philosopher Yang Xiong compiled a substantial list of words that varied from one area of China to another: He can be regarded as the world's first **dialectologist**, as he was the first person (to the best of our knowledge) who did an organized study of regional variation within a language.

Dialectologists concentrate on regional variation. During the period 1870–1960, **dialectology** developed into its modern form. There were several large-scale dialectological surveys in many places, including many parts of Europe, China and India. Traditional dialectology seeks out speakers whose speech is likely to be the most local. The large-scale study in England, the Survey of English Dialects, has been published in a number of forms, including as raw data, as an atlas (Orton et al., 1978), as a dictionary and, most recently, as part of the *Accents and Dialects* website hosted by the British Library. Often, researchers interview older rural men (less often women) who have always worked in agriculture in their home region, who have travelled little and who have not been educated to a high level. The questionnaire, such as the one used by the Survey of English Dialects, typically asks the respondents what words they use for particular concepts that are known to show variation in that particular language. For example, they might be asked what they call the place where cows are taken at night (in English, depending on the region, this could be a *byre, shippen, barn, cowshed* or *cowhouse*). They would also be asked to complete sentences to show grammatical differences. For example, the interviewer might say, *Yesterday I danced, today I . . .*, which could, in various parts of England, be completed with *am dancing / is dancing / be dancing / am adancing / be adancing.* In the early days of dialectology, before recordings could be made, the interviewer had to write down both words and pronunciation during the interview. After portable recording technology became available in the mid-twentieth century, recordings could be made, allowing transcriptions to be made later. In early dialectology, the interviews were often time consuming, taking several days to administer. They were very thorough and continue to provide important information about regional variation. Because the same questionnaire was used in several regions, these large-scale dialectological surveys allow the speech of one place to be compared to another, though obviously there are limits to this (e.g. not all communities keep cows, so there might not be a word for a shed in which they are sheltered).

The end products of dialectology include substantial publications listing all the findings, and overviews of various sorts, especially maps. Large-scale dialectology produces results of great complexity and interest, but dialectology can be done on a small scale too. Figure 4.1 shows the results

FIGURE 4.1 *Words for 'stream' in England (Gupta, 2005)*

from a small dialectological study of my own (Gupta, 2005), which shows variation in words for 'a small river': In England the word for this found all over the country is *stream*. For this study, there were only 119 respondents. The regional variation that I found in words other than *stream* (*burn, beck, brook* and *rhyne*) was very similar to that found in the Survey of English Dialects half a century earlier (Orton et al., 1978).

STANDARD DIALECTS

Until writing was developed about 6,000 years ago, all language was speech and it was all face-to-face. After that, until telephones developed in the late nineteenth century, writing was the only way in which communication through language could take place over long distances, beyond lines of sight and sound. Over time, writers developed the idea that there was a correct way to write a language. We can call this a **standard dialect**. Although many linguists would use the term 'dialect' for the standard **variety**, a standard is an unusual dialect because it is generally associated mostly with the written mode. However, in many languages, especially as literacy becomes widespread, users of the language develop the idea that there is a correct way to speak a language as well as a correct way to write it.

Reading and writing have to be taught, and writing is used to communicate over distances. As a result, all languages that are used in writing appear to develop a standard written form. When a language is first written down, it is often based, to some extent, on the speech patterns of a particular region, usually a region associated with the rulers. But writing systems are transmitted through school systems with great accuracy and, if there is political stability, a writing system might change little over time, so that in many languages (including English and Chinese) it is easy to read something written over 500 years ago. During those centuries, the spoken language, and especially its pronunciation, has changed a great deal, but the written language has changed less. Over time, a standard dialect gets further and further away from its regional origins. Standard English, for example, was based on the speech of educated people of the fifteenth century, and includes many features that were then associated with the East Midlands (the area near modern Cambridge). The spelling of English was closer to the pronunciation than it now is. Nowadays, however, Standard English is not associated with any regional dialect at all: It is just itself and has no region.

At some point after the development of a writing system, many languages do also develop a concept of a spoken standard dialect. The grammar and vocabulary of the standard dialect generally come to be seen as the 'best' way to speak the language. In many (but not all) languages, there also comes to be a standard accent, seen as the best way to pronounce the language. There is no such accent for English. A few languages develop a strict tradition about pronunciation, but most languages are much more relaxed about pronunciation than they are about grammar. Some languages have a tradition of having an official body to determine what is and what is not standard, while others do not. Schiffman (1996) discusses some of these important differences in linguistic culture. Learners of a language need to know the difference in notions of standards between their own language and the language they are learning. Some learners of English might be shocked to discover that there is no standard accent for English. If someone comes from a culture where there is a strong sense of a standard accent, they might be intolerant of regional variation in pronunciation, which can give offence to English users.

The standard dialect of English, Standard English, does not have a specific accent, but it has grammar, spelling and a set of words. Both in speech (with many accents) and in writing, it is a powerful worldwide dialect. We can see how strict it is in its grammar. For example, the inflections that are used to indicate tense and number on verbs, nouns and pronouns are strictly applied in Standard English (see Chapter 2). Although DIVE has two past tenses in Standard English (*dived* and *dove*), nearly all other verbs have only one past tense form throughout Standard English (*was, had, forgot, kept, sat*). Other dialects of English differ grammatically from Standard English. For example *I am dancing* is Standard English and *I be adancing* is not; *I did it* is Standard English and *I done it* is not; *I don't have any* is Standard English and *I don't have none* is not. On the other hand, there are many ways of pronouncing *dance* in Standard English. Standard English is an unusual dialect because it is not associated with a particular accent, unlike other dialects.

So important are standard dialects, that in many linguistic cultures they are felt to be the language itself. Speakers of different dialects who learn to read and write in the same standard dialect are generally felt to be speaking the same language. New standard dialects can develop from what was once a dialect. Old standard dialects can stop being used, so that what were once two languages can become two dialects of the same language.

This issue of where one language stops and another begins is related to language policy; I will not be discussing it in this chapter (see Chapter 9). The best way to find out what language someone is speaking is to ask them, but do not expect that everyone will answer in the same way: There is no hard and fast linguistic way to determine whether two similar ways of speaking are dialects of the same language or are different languages.

SOCIAL VARIATION

There is another kind of variation, however, which dialectology now studies in addition to regional variation: This is **social variation**, linguistic variation according to social characteristics other than region, especially social class, age and gender. Dialectology was revolutionized in the 1960s by the father of modern **sociolinguistics**, William Labov. Sociolinguistics is the study of how language works in a social context. At the time when sociolinguistics first was identified as a branch of linguistics, Labov did ground-breaking research that changed the way in which linguistic variation was studied. His findings are still important, and the methodology that he developed is a basic tool for sociolinguists studying language variation. Studies using Labov's methodologies are often referred to as **variationist sociolinguistics, social dialectology** or **Labovian sociolinguistics**.

Other social characteristics intersect with regional variation. Not everyone from the same place speaks in the same way. Every human being has multiple identities, and each aspect of identity can be expressed in a person's speech. For example, the way we speak can indicate social class, gender, ethnicity, religion or educational attainment as well as regional origins. Any difference that is socially important is likely to be reflected in speech.

Traditional dialectology focussed on regional variation, and not on differences between people from the same place. Traditional dialectologists did not examine the speech of people of higher social class or the speech of those who had a high level of education, because, in many societies, the speech of more prestigious groups does not vary as much from one region to another as does the speech of the less prestigious groups. This is one of the results of literacy and of the development of a standard dialect. Indeed, the spread of education was one of the things that inspired nineteenth-century dialectologists to undertake their research: They thought that dialectal variation would be destroyed by the increase in literacy. They were not quite correct: Dialectal variation continues to flourish, and new dialectal variation continues to develop (in the English of Australia, for example). But the fact that so many speakers now know standard dialects is important in helping us to understand why and how people from the same place do not speak in the same way as each other, and in understanding why an individual does not always speak in the same way.

Whatever the language, wherever the place, social factors will be reflected in the speech of the people. There appears to be nowhere in the world where everyone in the same community speaks identically. It also appears to be the case that individuals do not always speak in the same way: There is variation within the individual as well as variation from one individual to another. The patterns that are found vary from one linguistic culture to another, but there is always variation between individuals and within the individual.

In some languages, educated speakers use a regional dialect alongside the standard dialect, depending on what they are doing. In other languages, educated speakers always use the standard dialect and do not use a regional dialect. Chinese speakers from Guangdong are likely to speak Cantonese (a regional dialect) as well as Mandarin (also known as Putonghua), which has, in the last century or so, become the standard dialect for Chinese as a whole. Some speakers of German will make daily switches between their regional dialect (such as Bavarian) and High German (Hochdeutsch), which is considered to be the standard for the country as a whole. In some parts of the English-using world (such as Jamaica, Singapore, Glasgow, Lagos), many people use two quite distinct dialects of English, with different grammar as well as pronunciation, switching between the local dialect of English (Patwa, Singlish, Scots or Nigerian Pidgin English) and Standard English depending on the social context. In all these cases, the difference between the local dialect and Standard English is so great that some people argue that the local variety is a separate language, and not a dialect of English.

There are, however, many parts of the English-using world (such as New York, Leeds, Sydney and Delhi) where English speakers are unlikely to move from one distinct dialect to another. They vary their accent, but not their grammar. It is this variation in accent that is the main subject of research for variationist sociolinguists. Labovian research begins with the observation that, in any particular place, some alternative pronunciations have higher prestige than others.

There is no single standard accent for English. English users of high prestige speak with a wide range of accents. In any given region where English is spoken, some accents are seen as more prestigious than others, but the linguistic features that signal prestige are not the same everywhere. For example, few Americans can distinguish the social meaning of the different accents of England, and vice versa. Confusingly, the whole world seems to share the idea that there are 'right' ways of pronouncing individual words, even though different pronunciations can signal different social meanings to different speakers. English speakers might accept a whole range of ways of pronouncing the vowels of *cat*, or of *know*, but they can be dismissive of someone who begins *chaos* with the same sound as *church*. English speakers might not criticize someone for the way they say the vowel of *take*, but they might get very upset about whether or not someone has a /h/ sound at the beginning of the name of the letter *H*. It is accent variation in speech sounds (such as the vowels of *cat* or *know*) that variationist sociolinguists study, rather than the pronunciation of individual words.

One result of the development of literacy is that, in many languages, the way in which speakers from different places speak converges. Speakers of high prestige from different places might speak more similarly to each other than to less prestigious people from their own community. The less prestige someone has, the stronger the regionality of their speech is likely to be. This has been known for some time, which is why traditional dialectologists chose to interview farm workers with little education. The new style of dialectology that began with Labov, variationist sociolinguistics, deals with urban as well as rural dwellers, and with the educated as well as the uneducated. Labov's main research area is the East Coast of the USA: Variationist sociolinguistics works best in those places (like New York, Norwich and Melbourne) where speakers change their pronunciation of speech sounds in quite subtle ways. It does not work as well in places (like Lagos or Singapore) where speakers switch between dialects that differ a great deal in grammar. Variationist sociolinguistics uses the idea that accents can be ranked in terms of their prestige, and it focuses on how individual speakers within a single community use their own sense of prestige by varying their speech in a way that shows their group membership. The emphasis for these dialectologists is less on regional variety or on attempts to identify non-standard features, and more on understanding the social factors which influence linguistic variation in a single place. The careful methods that Labov developed were designed to study variation within a community – not to make comparison across regions.

Labov began his fieldwork as a doctoral student in Martha's Vineyard, then a quiet island off the New England coast, beginning to be the popular holiday place it now is. He went on to undertake a major study of the speech of New York's Lower East Side. In these studies, he developed a methodology for studying dialectal variation within a single community. The basic Labovian methodology, as laid out in his report on the New York study (Labov, 1966), is as follows:

1 The researchers already have some idea (perhaps gleaned from traditional dialectological work, or from personal knowledge of the community) about what linguistic features show variation in this community. They select which features they plan to study. The researchers must be sure that they are able to compare things which have the same meaning and that the feature they study has high frequency. For example, in a particular community (such as New York and Singapore) speakers sometimes have an [θ] (a hissing sound made with the tongue between the teeth) in words like *thin* and *three* and sometimes have a [t] (the same sound as they have in *tin* and *tree*). The meaning of *think* and *three* is the same whether they begin it with

a [θ] or a [t]. Features that show this kind of variation are the **linguistic variables,** and most will relate to pronunciation of speech sounds in a set of words. The reason that most linguistic variables are in the area of pronunciation is (a) because this is the main area of variation in language; (b) because a variation in pronunciation is always going to have high frequency; and (c) because variations in pronunciation of speech sounds do not change meaning.

2 Each linguistic variable has more than one possible realization in the community: These are the **linguistic variants**. The variants must be rankable in terms of prestige: Usually this is something the researchers are already aware of because of their local knowledge ([θ] is more prestigious than [t]), though the ranking of variants can emerge from the results. In Labovian studies, the names of the variables are written in an adaptation of ordinary spelling, in round parentheses. The variants are written in square brackets, in phonetic symbols. The variable I have used as an example would be the (th) variable and the variants I have mentioned are [θ] and [t].

3 Next, the researchers select people they are going to interview in such a way that there are clear differences in their social characteristics. The social differences between the speakers are the **social variables**. They are likely to include socio-economic status (calculated in a variety of ways), gender and age. It is important that the researchers can explain how they have selected their respondents so that the nature of the sample is understood. The way in which respondents are selected will affect the generalizability of the study. The population base could be any size: It could be a whole city but it could also be a smaller community, such as a single school, or a family. The researchers discard respondents who were not born and raised in the selected location. They might also discard other respondents, such as those of certain ethnic backgrounds, bilinguals or people under or over a certain age.

4 The researchers administer and record a **sociolinguistic interview**: This is a particular style of interview used in Labovian dialectology, which elicits, at the same time, speech and social information from the respondents. In this interview, the researchers get full information on the respondents' social characteristics (gender, age, education, income, occupation, etc.). Their spoken answers provide data for the sociolinguistic analysis. During the interview, the researchers also make sure that they use a range of **styles**. 'Style' has a particular, and specific, meaning in variationist sociolinguistics, it refers to different

levels of formality. A Labovian sociolinguistic interview includes different activities that can be ranked in terms of their formality. The most formal style would be reading words on a list and the least formal would be talking about something that makes the respondent feel strong emotions. Labov's idea was that in the more formal styles (such as reading a word list), more attention is paid to speech, while in the more casual styles (such as the body of the interview, and the sections where the respondent felt strong emotion), less attention is paid to speech. Up to five different styles can be used in a Labovian interview. Labov predicted that the speech used when the respondent feels strong emotion would be in the person's least prestigious style, which he calls the 'vernacular'. Labovian studies use various questions to generate this emotional speech. In his New York research, Labov asked respondents whether they had ever been in danger of death, but this question has not been suitable in other cultures. Other researchers have asked respondents to talk about something funny that happened to them, to talk about something from their childhood or to talk about favourite foods. In other branches of linguistics, 'style' has a wider meaning. Labovian sociolinguistic interviews can often be completed in about an hour and are much less time consuming than traditional dialectological interviews. Respondents generally find them enjoyable.

5   The researchers use the recordings as data. The content in the interview is used to classify respondents in terms of the social variables. Researchers use the sound of the speech in the recording to determine respondents' score in terms of the linguistic variables. They count how many times each speaker uses each variable in each style (occurrences). Every time a variable is used, the researchers identify the variant. If there are two variants as in my example with (th), a score of one is given to the least prestigious variant [t] and a score of zero to the most prestigious [θ] (or sometimes vice versa). They then add up the score and calculate the rate (the score divided by occurrences).

6   The hardest work comes next. When the scores for all the variables have been calculated, the researchers have to interpret their results and try to understand what the results mean in terms of the relationship between the social variables and the linguistic variables in this community. There will be patterns, but they might be very complex. In most communities there will be large differences relating to socio-economic status, but in many communities other social variables will

be of huge importance, such as gender or age, which make patterns hard to identify and sometimes controversial.

Labov's methods provided a scientific methodology for the study of linguistic variation, especially for the study of variation in accent. The results are usually supplied either as tables of rates, variable by variable, or as graphs showing the same data. Figure 4.2 is an example of how data can be presented. It is a redrawn version of one of the original graphs from Labov's work on New York (Labov, 1966, p. 156), which I have relabelled to make it easier to understand out of context.

The graph shows the rates at which variants other than [θ] were used: These other variants were mostly [t], though [f] was also found. The pattern shown here is of a straightforward **sociolinguistic variable**. All groups of speakers show variation: All groups, in all styles, use [θ] sometimes, but not always. There is a clear pattern. The more informally people speak, the less they use [θ]. And the lower their socio-economic status, the less they use [θ].

Over and over again, variationist sociolinguistics shows that each individual draws on a variety of speech sounds. The more prestigious people are, the greater proportion of high-prestige variants they use. But most speakers mix their use of the more and the less prestigious variants depending on what they are doing.

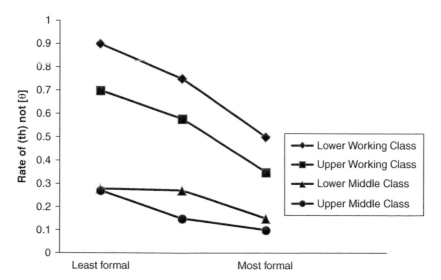

FIGURE 4.2 *The (th) variable: Four class groups and three styles (adapted from Labov, 1966)*

If you look at William Labov's Home Page, you can find out more about his research and methods. The work he did in the 1960s has been the basis of a great deal of research by him and by others, and has become increasingly developed over time.

Variationist sociolinguistics was designed to cope with linguistic variation in native speakers of a language who were living in highly literate communities where most people speak the same language. In communities with extensive bilingualism (see Chapter 8), or where literacy in the native language is low, it can be hard or impossible to identify variables that show the expected pattern. Labov's methodology is not an appropriate methodology for all communities.

One problem for the teacher is that it can be hard to understand and use the concepts of prestige and linguistic variation. In the case of the (th) variable in English, the same variant, [θ], is the most prestigious variant all over the world. This is not the case with many other variables though. The way in which hearers attribute prestige to a particular accent is complex. Each place where a language is used has its own idea of what speech sounds have the most prestige. In some contexts, some foreign accents might be perceived as more prestigious than most local accents, especially if the message a hearer gets is that the speaker is highly intelligent as a result of being a foreign learner. This brings us to the issue of the complex social messages embedded in language variation, including how people use and understand language to express identity.

EXPRESSING IDENTITY

There are two ways of thinking about identity: who you *are* and who you *want* to be. The way people speak is not simply the inevitable outcome of where they were born and into what social class. People take an active part in choosing how they speak, both consciously and unconsciously. We learn new languages if we need to, and we learn new dialects and accents too. Many of us take on a range of linguistic identities, just as we take on a range of social roles. Writers also express personal identity through language, but most sociolinguists focus on speech.

Sociolinguists since the 1960s have developed several ways of looking at the patterns of how speakers convey their identity in the way they use a language. The linguistic theory that I find useful was developed by R. B. Le Page, a pioneer in identity sociolinguistics, whose work on Jamaican English in the 1950s caused him to reflect on how speakers express their identity by the choices they make in speech. His **Acts of Identity** theory (developed over many years, but published in full as Le Page and Tabouret-Keller, 1985) can be summarized as the idea that, when we speak, we do our best to give the people we are speaking to the impression that we are the kind of person we want them to think we are. The most obvious example, which works in all languages, is in gender. Most people want to be perceived as being either male or female. One of the ways in which we do this is through pitch. The pitch differences between male and female voices are larger than the biological differences explain: Men and boys tend to pitch their voices lower than expected and women and girls tend to pitch their voices higher than expected. Some cultures (such as Japan) have a particularly large pitch difference between men and women, but everywhere it is clear that people who identify as men want to be heard as being men and people who identify as women want to be heard as being women.

A number of other sociolinguists have, in various ways, explored how speakers try to project their identity to others, some using a Labovian approach, and others using a mixture of methods. Coupland (2007) gives a summary of these approaches, and many examples from his own work and that of others. At all times, we are expressing an identity as we speak. We are doing our best to tell our hearers about ourselves. Within one language, we usually choose from a limited repertoire, and, unless we have created a totally new biography for ourselves, that repertoire is usually linked to our actual origins and history.

One of the ways in which we express identity is in the way we choose between linguistic variants. For example, someone from New York who wants to sound particularly rich and highly educated on a specific occasion might make sure to use [θ] at a high rate, and avoid [t] in pronouncing the (th) variable in words like *thin* and *three*.

Another way in which we express identity is to try to speak more like the person to whom we are speaking. Howard Giles (1973) called this 'Accommodation'. The speech of two people tends to converge when they want to express **solidarity**, a friendly sense of unity. We can also use choices from our personal repertoire in order to be aggressive or express a sense of superiority to the person we are speaking to.

Speakers who commonly use more than one language choose alternatives within their repertoire very clearly by **codeswitching**: moving between one language and another (see Chapter 8). For example, an English-Yoruba bilingual who meets a Yoruba stranger for a business meeting might start to conduct the business in English but then add a few sentences in Yoruba to signal shared experience and give a more friendly feeling. It can be harder to see that such Acts of Identity are happening when only one language is involved. Nevertheless, speakers use a range of pronunciations, words and grammatical structures in order to signal to others (they hope) who they are and who they want to be. And who they are and want to be varies from time to time and place to place. We want to be different people for different people.

This approach to variation can be called **identity sociolinguistics**: Eckert (2008) calls it the Third Wave of sociolinguistics – Labov being the first – but identity sociolinguistics has developed at the same time as Labovian sociolinguistics, sometimes drawing on insights that did not come from Labovian sociolinguistics. Identity sociolinguists focus on the way in which people (consciously and unconsciously) choose linguistic variants in order to express an identity, either real or assumed. Interviews are seldom used. The data of identity sociolinguistics is usually naturally occurring conversation of people within their normal social settings. Such conversations are recorded and transcribed and then analysed in detail. Analysis may be quantitative, involving calculating the proportion of variants, or it may involve the close examination of a single form in a conversation. The focus is on speakers as active creators of their own identity, and of collective identities.

We can even pretend (especially in writing) to be someone we are not. We can be playful, taking on identities that don't belong to us, either for humour, or to signal that we would like to have membership of a group, or to show the warmth of solidarity. Examples of this are easy to find in both speech and writing, and usually involve using some characteristic words or structures of a dialect other than the standard dialect, which are used alongside the standard dialect. Sociolinguists have used various terms to describe this pattern of behaviour, including **emblematic**, **indexical**, **criterial** and **stylization**. Here is someone who enjoyed a holiday in northwest Scotland, and makes a comment in an online guest book. (I have italicized the sections in Scots.)

> *Fit like!! Whit an afae bonnie website! Fermer Livingstone is a richt braw mannie! We hope he kens fur aboots the kettle is (jist in case Anne's awa tae the dancin')* for our next visit to the most beautiful island in the world! (by the way – when will the *tatties* be ready, and *keep yer bull awa fae the caravan*!!!) Seriously though...... the website is excellent and we can't wait to be back on Lismore. (Isle of Lismore Community Website, 2001, <www.isleoflismore.com/guest_book/2001_guest_book.htm>)

This writer actually tells us that her intent is humorous, as she signals her final, Standard English, comment, with 'seriously'. We do not know whether she *speaks* Scots or not, but she uses Scots here, in writing, to signal solidarity, expressing a Scottish identity in common with the place that she loved and the people who made her welcome.

Whenever we speak, in whatever languages we know, we project an identity. The effect on our listeners will vary depending on their experiences, knowledge and prejudices and as a result the effect might be quite different from the effect we thought we would have. Anyone who has travelled the English-using world will realize that speakers of English often cannot tell where you are from. In Australia I am often asked if I am Irish or from London; in England most speakers can hear that I am from the North of England. We all make fine distinctions in the sociolinguistic variables of the places that matter to us, but we may be oblivious to other communities' sociolinguistic variables.

Teachers and learners need to realize that it is impossible to speak a language without giving an impression of who you are: Learners too can reflect on what identity they *want* to convey. There are schools and universities in Northern and Eastern Europe that train their students to replicate a particular English accent, usually one from the USA or England. Such training does not take into account the types of social variation discussed here: It is based on the assumption that there is a single-best high-prestige accent in the USA and another in England, and that this high-prestige accent will be the best for learners. A result might be that successful students who visit England give a strange message to their local listeners, such as a 20-year-old Polish student sounding like an elderly aristocrat. Teachers and students alike need to reflect on what effect is desirable. Students who are proud to be, for example, Polish, might want people to hear them as being highly educated and good in English, but still Polish. They might not *want* to be mistaken for an English person if they want to project a Polish identity.

Learners of many languages are likely to encounter written and spoken non-standard dialects in literature (mostly in the representation of speech), and in song lyrics. Learners of English will see and hear non-standard English of all kinds as soon as they begin to communicate in English, either face-to-face or online. They need to know what non-standard dialects look and sound like, and in what contexts they are appropriate.

RELEVANCE TO EDUCATIONAL SETTINGS

Linguistic variation is an inevitable part of language use. It is part of how we tell other people who we are and who we want to be. Whatever language you are teaching, you will need to learn about linguistic variation in the language that you teach. You will need to prepare your students to cope with linguistic variation in a way that will help them to interact with its speakers and writers.

I hope you will want to teach them in a way that does not develop prejudice against speakers of some varieties.

The standard dialect is important and should be the main focus. In most languages, it is the most widely used dialect, both in terms of where it is used and for what functions. In most languages, there is little variation within the written standard dialect. Because of its prestige and usefulness, the standard dialect is nearly always the dialect traditionally taught to learners. However, teachers and students should know that there is always linguistic variation. Therefore, it is best to use terms such as 'standard', 'not standard' and 'other dialect' rather than 'right', 'correct' or 'wrong'.

Only the most advanced learners would ever want to use grammatical structures from other dialects. Learners will see and hear dialects other than the standard one, however, and will need to be informed about them as soon as they start using the language. This is certainly true of English, where non-standard dialects are widely used in the media, especially in music and in online communication. They need to know the contexts in which non-standard dialects are and are not appropriate. Think about the variation (in pronunciation, grammar and vocabulary) that the students will encounter in both speech and writing. If a student writes something non-standard that you think they have learnt outside of class, discuss it with them. Students will be confused if they see or hear language forms that you then tell them are wrong. But if you tell them that this is part of language variation, they will understand.

In many languages, especially ones spoken over a wide area, there is great variation in pronunciation. Some languages have a standard accent, but others do not. Beginners should be given a consistent model for the speech sounds of the language, if possible, but, once they are past the early stages, they will have to learn to understand a range of accents. Whatever language you are teaching, you should encourage students to be tolerant of variation in accent. They should not regard speakers from certain regions as being in error. In languages with a wide range of accents, like English, you should not spend too much time on producing a perfect imitation of an accent. Advanced students should learn to understand a range of accents, and they should also learn to identify some of the common variations from one accent to another.

DISCUSSION AND REFLECTION QUESTIONS

1   Do you speak a language in which you move between the standard dialect and another dialect? If so, when do you use which? If not, do you know anyone who does this?

2 Think about your own pronunciation in any language. Identify a sociolinguistic variable. What variants do you use? Are there any other variants of the same variable in your community?

3 Remember yourself in a particular situation (such as on a train, or in a shop), when you met and talked to a particular stranger (a man? a woman? how old?). What sort of person did you want that stranger to think you were? Why? Can you now reflect on how your speech might have changed as a result of what you wanted the person to think of you?

RECOMMENDED READING AND VIEWING

The British Library has brought together a number of resources on accents and dialects in (mostly) England. There are old and new recordings to listen to, transcriptions to look at while you listen and explanations. It's a complicated site, because it is so rich, but well worth exploring.

Accents and Dialects. London: British Library Board. Available at: http://sounds.bl.uk/Accents-and-dialects/

You can read more about Yang Xiong and his dialectological work, 方言 (*Fāng Yán*) online. There is a good introduction at:

Colvin, A. (2005), Yang Xiong (53 BCE–18 CE). *Internet Encyclopedia of Philosophy*. Available at: www.iep.utm.edu/yangxion/

Those who read Chinese can browse the full text:

方言 (Fang Yan). 中國哲學書電子化計劃 (*Chinese Text Project*). Available at: http://ctext.org/fang-yan/zh

It is difficult to learn phonetics without face-to-face instruction, but Ladefoged's book should help you understand some basics about this important tool of linguistics.

Ladefoged, P. (2006), *Vowels and Consonants* (5th edn). Boston, MA: Thomson/ Wadsworth Publishers.

A UCLA (University of California, Los Angeles) website for this book includes an IPA chart on which you can click to hear the sounds represented by the symbols. See:
www.phonetics.ucla.edu/course/contents.html

William Labov maintains a lively website that allows you to look through the development of his important work and see what he is working on now. You might be surprised to see that some of what he does is more like traditional dialectology.

Labov, W. (2012), *William Labov: Home Page*. Available at: www.ling. upenn.edu/~wlabov/

If you want to read more about the current identity-based approach to linguistic variation, Coupland's is an excellent account.

Coupland, N. (2007), *Style: Language Variation and Identity*. Cambridge: Cambridge University Press.

5

How Do Children Learn Language?

Theres Grüter

INTRODUCTION

As educators and parents, we like to take credit for the achievements of the children in our care. And often this is justified. A child's health, for example, is greatly impacted by the diet we provide. Yet at the same time, there are biological factors, such as a genetically conditioned inability to produce insulin, leading to childhood diabetes, that are clearly beyond our control. Much the same is true for language development. The goal of this chapter is to introduce you to the major social and cognitive factors that contribute to human language development. The chapter focuses on language acquisition in early childhood in a variety of learning situations, including monolingual and bilingual environments, as well as children with language learning difficulties.

As educators and parents, we can and must provide a child with a rich language environment through meaningful and age-appropriate interactions. Experiential and environmental factors are important contributors to the development of language: A child raised in an English-speaking environment learns English, a child raised in a Cantonese-speaking environment learns Cantonese, and a child with sufficient meaningful interactions in both English and Cantonese naturally learns both. (See cultural transmission, Chapter 1.)

Recent research has shown that experiential factors influence language development even beyond which language(s) a child does or does not acquire. In a landmark study, Hart and Risley (1995) recorded interactions in the homes of English-speaking families from various socio-economic backgrounds in the USA over a period of three years. One of their most striking findings was the variability in the sheer amount of speech children experienced, with children from professional families hearing an estimated 30 million more words over their first three years of life than children living in poverty. Importantly, these differences in experience correlated with the number of words children knew at age 3: 3-year-olds from higher socio-economic backgrounds, who had experienced richer language environments, used over 1,000 different words, whereas their peers from less advantaged backgrounds produced only half as many. What is more, these differences in early language experience were predictive of academic achievement years later in elementary school. In other words, the children who experienced more language directed at them in early childhood had a larger vocabulary and tended to do better in school.

The fact that language experience matters is even more obvious in the case of children who grow up in bi- or multilingual environments. Barbara Pearson and her colleagues studied the language development of infants raised in a Spanish/English bilingual environment in Florida (Pearson et al., 1997). Through interviews with parents and caregivers, they estimated the proportion of time each child was exposed to Spanish versus English. They also looked at how many Spanish words and how many English words each child knew. Not surprisingly, they found that children with more exposure to Spanish knew more Spanish than English words, and children with more interactions in English knew more English than Spanish words. Thus at least with regard to vocabulary knowledge, experience clearly matters. Much less is known about the relation between environmental factors and other aspects of linguistic development, such as knowledge of grammar, an issue that is being investigated in current research. (For more on bilingual development, see Chapter 8.)

On the other hand, there are children who struggle with language despite rich language experience and caring environments. In some cases, this is due to a known medical condition, such as Down Syndrome, which affects cognitive development more broadly. For a child with Down Syndrome, language is one of many abilities impacted. Yet in many other cases, there is no obvious explanation for why a child is lagging behind her peers in language development. There are children who have no known medical condition and do well on non-verbal cognitive measures, but who fail to meet major milestones in language development. (I will discuss language milestones in more detail below.) These children perform well below expectations for their age on standardized language tests. They are often diagnosed as having **Specific Language Impairment (SLI)**, a developmental disorder that is quite common. It has been estimated to affect about 5–7 per cent of preschool-aged children.

The causes of SLI are still poorly understood, but research has shown that a child is more likely to have SLI if someone else in the family also has it, suggesting that there is a genetic component to it. Children diagnosed with SLI are normally advised to see a speech-language therapist. This is important because although these children have normal cognitive abilities, persistent weaknesses in language development may affect their academic performance more broadly, since a delay in oral language development can lead to difficulties with reading, a critical ability for scholastic achievement (see Chapter 7). Fortunately, in many cases, children diagnosed with SLI eventually catch up with their peers in terms of language development, sometimes even by the time they start school. This often happens with the help of a speech-language therapist. In other cases, difficulties persist into the school years and possibly never fully resolve. Some researchers call the former 'specific language delay', and only the latter 'specific language impairment'. Yet when a young child looks like she is struggling with language, it is difficult to know whether this is just a temporary issue or whether it presents a more persistent problem. Researchers are currently trying to understand how the two could be distinguished early on so that they can know best how to help these children.

The existence of genetically conditioned language disorders is not the only indication that biological factors, in addition to experiential ones, play an important role in language acquisition. Let's consider the converse scenario: a child with intact cognitive and biological prerequisites for language learning, but an environment that, for one reason or another, provides only impoverished language experience. An example of such a case is a boy named Simon (pseudonym), whose development was followed by Singleton and Newport (2004) for a period of about seven years, starting around age 2. Simon was born deaf, and his parents communicated with him in American Sign Language (ASL). ASL, like other sign languages used by deaf communities around the world, has all the unique 'design features' of a human language (see Chapter 1), but instead of using sounds it relies on combinations of hand motions and facial expression to convey meaning. Simon's parents, having learned ASL only later in life, were fluent but not fully proficient users of the language. For example, they only rarely, and sometimes incorrectly, produced more complex grammatical constructions in ASL. Simon had no interactions with native ASL signers, which could have provided the full-fledged linguistic experience available to most children. Singleton and Newport observed that right around the age when children typically begin to use more complex sentences, Simon started combining the limited resources from the language he had learned from his parents to produce more complex sentences, structures that were not present in the input he had received. Simon thus went beyond what he had experienced to effectively invent parts of his grammar. His story illustrates the astonishing resilience on the part of the child not only to acquire language in a less than optimal linguistic environment, but also to approximate developmental milestones characteristic of typical development.

The story of Simon is only one case study, but it is by no means an exception. Similar observations have been made in areas where speakers from different language backgrounds came together, often as a result of trade, and initially developed a simplified language for basic communication, which linguists call a 'pidgin'. Importantly, when these pidgin speakers had children, this next generation of speakers developed a language with far more complexity than the pidgin they were exposed to, a language linguists call a 'creole', which is comparable in function and complexity to any other human language. In a paper aptly entitled 'On the acquisition of native speakers by a language', Sankoff and LaBerge (1973) observed that this increase in complexity in creole languages is brought about predominantly by children. In other words, as the children are exposed to and use the pidgin, they create a more complex grammar. This leads to the development of a new language, a creole. Thus just like Simon, children of pidgin-speaking parents go beyond the input they receive to create a full-fledged human language.

Observations like these suggest that a predisposition to learn language is part of our genetic endowment as members of the human species. We cannot help but acquire language. The precise nature and evolution of this predisposition is a matter of intense debate among linguists and psychologists. Yet most people would agree that neither biology nor the environment alone are enough to explain how we come to learn language in its full glory. As Lila Gleitman, a leading researcher in the field, famously put it in a documentary about language acquisition almost two decades ago: 'I take it that this is the question of modern linguistics: how much of language does a child have to learn, and how much is built in?' (Searchinger, 1995). We are still humblingly far away from having good answers to this question.

SOME MAJOR MILESTONES: AN OVERVIEW

Around halfway into their first year of life, after several months of producing various gurgling and cooing noises, babies spontaneously start experimenting with language-like sounds by repetitively stringing together consonants and vowels into something that sounds like *bababa* or *dadada*. This is called **babbling** and marks the first important milestone in children's productive use of language. Babbling is a phenomenon that babies from all cultures engage in, including those who are deaf or hard of hearing. Babies whose main interactions are with speakers of a sign language like ASL have been observed to start producing repetitive hand motions consisting of very basic aspects of adult signs around that same age. This phenomenon has been called 'manual babbling', and it suggests that babbling is a universal stage in child language development. Closer to the child's first birthday, these syllable strings typically start getting more varied and creative (*agagu*, *badaga*), and may show signs of sounding more like the language(s) the child is learning in terms of specific sounds and stress patterns.

All this sets the stage for the next great step in language development: the first word. Most people (and textbooks) expect babies to say their first word somewhere around their first birthday. This is true, on average. However, it is important to be aware that although children around the world follow a remarkably similar course in language development, there is also great variability as to when exactly they reach each milestone. Thus while it is true for many children that they will produce their first word around 12 months of age, some do so as early as 9 or 10 months and others wait until they are 17 or 18 months old. There is generally no need for concern if a child does not speak until after 18 months, although it is important to pay attention to whether an 18-month-old in this situation seems to understand speech addressed to her. If babies around that age show little evidence of engaging in interaction or understanding words, a thorough assessment of their hearing is typically recommended as a first evaluative step.

Similarly, there is a great deal of variation in when children reach the next major milestone in language development: putting two words together, as in *more milk* or *eat cookie*. For most children, this happens around 18 months of age, or when they have about 50 words in their productive vocabulary. Yet for some, it happens as early as 15 months, while others wait until their second birthday. Anything within this range is considered 'normal' (a notion we will consider a little more closely in the next section), just as it is normal for some children to walk or get their first teeth a little earlier or later than others. If by 26 months a child is still not putting two words together, further evaluation is typically advised.

After several months in what is called the two-word stage, children's utterances gradually become longer, but are still quite different from adult sentences. A child at this stage will say things like *I got horn* or *doggie go out*. This has been called **telegraphic speech** because it resembles the language that was used for writing telegrams, in which each word cost money, and therefore words that were not immediately necessary to convey important content were omitted. Similarly, the telegraphic speech we typically see in children around 2 to 2.5 years of age is characterized by the omission of inflection (e.g. third person /-s/) and function words (e.g. articles like *the*). Yet as we will see below, despite these omissions, children's early multiword utterances resemble adult sentences in important ways.

Once children start producing multiword utterances, they rapidly progress to acquire more complex grammatical structures (such as negation, question formation and inflection) throughout the preschool years. This does not happen without errors along the way. Certain types of errors are very much part of normal development, and we will look at some of them in more detail below. By the time they start kindergarten, children have acquired most of the grammar of their language(s). Yet their language development is far from complete. Some more complex and less frequent constructions, such as passives or relative clauses, are typically not fully mastered until well after the preschool years. Children continue to learn more words as they expand their experiences, and particularly as they learn to read and write. They also continue to learn how to structure and organize their talk, how to adapt their talk to different people and social situations and how to deal with common rhetorical devices such as irony and metaphor. There is no endpoint to language acquisition. Language is not a machine that is assembled and runs when complete. Just like the living organisms within which it resides, language continues to develop and evolve, shaped by constant dynamic interaction with the social environments in which it is situated.

HOW DO WE KNOW WHAT IS 'NORMAL'?

The age points and ranges for the major developmental milestones presented in the previous section are based on a cumulative body of research conducted over many decades. Much of the early research in the field was based on evidence from a small number of children, typically monolingual English-speakers from well-educated middle- to upper-class families, not seldom the children of the researchers themselves. One might rightfully wonder whether this kind of evidence is truly representative of child language development more generally. Fortunately, much progress has been made over the past two decades through the development of relatively simple standardized measures, which have allowed for the collection and analysis of data from thousands of children from various social and economic backgrounds. The *MacArthur-Bates Communicative Development Inventories* (Fenson et al., 2006) is one such instrument, and we owe much of what we know about what is 'normal' in early language development to it. The CDI, as it is commonly known, consists of carefully constructed lists of several hundred words, and parents or caregivers are asked to check which words on this list a child says or understands. While an individual parent's estimate of what their child might say or understand at a given point in time may not be 100 per cent accurate, combined data from thousands of these questionnaires provide us with an excellent indication of the range of what we might consider 'normal'. CDI norms also provide useful benchmarks for assessing the development of an individual child, and are widely used in clinical practice. The CDI was originally developed for English, but has now been adapted, linguistically and culturally, to over 50 different languages and dialects.

Once children move beyond the one-word stage, quantifying their language development becomes more difficult. Brown (1973) introduced a widely used measure of grammatical development called **mean length of utterance**, or **MLU**. MLU is calculated by counting the number of morphemes, the smallest meaningful units of language, in a child's speech, and averaging that number over a total of 100 consecutive utterances. For example *two balls* consists of three morphemes (*two+ball+s*). (See also Chapter 2.) A child with an MLU of 3 produces, on average, utterances of this length and complexity. MLU has proven to be an excellent reflection of a child's stage in early grammatical development. Yet its calculation involves the recording of a representative speech sample, transcription as well as analysis. This process is both time consuming and difficult to standardize, which is why the use of MLU in educational and clinical assessment has been limited. Instead, language assessment for educational or clinical purposes in the (pre)school years typically involves the use of specially developed standardized tests designed to probe children's abilities in various subdomains of language use (sounds, words, sentences) in both production and comprehension.

Until very recently, the vast majority of the research that has informed our understanding of child language acquisition has come from children exposed to a single language. This reflects the predominantly Western, Anglo-Saxon culture from which much of this research has emerged. Yet it has been estimated that more than half of the world's population is bi- or multilingual. How do the milestones we have identified so far apply to children who grow up in multilingual environments? People who have grown up in monolingual environments themselves often intuitively believe that it must take longer for a child to learn two languages at the same time. After all, there is twice as much language to be acquired. So should we expect bilingual children to be delayed in their language development? This is not an easy question to answer, and we must be very careful about what we mean by 'language'. We can look, for example, at the number of words a child knows in a given language. If we compare a monolingual (e.g. English) and a bilingual (e.g. English/Cantonese) child on this measure, it is likely (but not guaranteed) that the monolingual child will know more English words than her bilingual peer at the same age. Yet does this mean that the bilingual child is lagging behind in *language* development, or just in the size of her *English vocabulary*? Importantly, if we add the number of words bilingual children are reported to know in *both* of their languages, those totals tend to equal, on average, the number of words that monolingual children typically know in their one language at the same age. Moreover, when we look at the major milestones identified so far – the emergence of babbling, first words and first two-word combinations – it has been found that bilingual children generally reach them well within the (wide) range of what is considered normal in monolingual development. All this suggests that acquiring multiple languages at the same time is well within a child's capacity, and does not lead to delays in language development overall (see Chapter 8).

At the same time, it is important to remember that few bilingual children experience their two languages in comparable quantity and quality. For example, a child might hear one language from only a single person in her life and only for a limited number of hours per week, whereas she might have many more interactions in the other language. In this case, it will not be surprising to find one language develop more slowly, and perhaps to a more limited degree of proficiency, than the other. In cases such as these, estimating what is 'normal' development is very difficult because it is hard to know what should serve as a basis for comparison. In general, it is recommended that a bilingual child always be assessed in both languages, and that her abilities in the stronger language are taken as more indicative of her general language development. In practice, this is not always easy.

In the last two sections, we have identified major milestones in early language development, looked briefly at how language development may be assessed and quantified for research as well as educational and clinical purposes and considered how what we know based on monolingual language development extends to children growing up with two or more languages. In the following sections, we will delve a little deeper into looking at the many factors that contribute towards the amazing feat of acquiring a human language.

THE JOURNEY INTO LANGUAGE: WHAT HAPPENS BEFORE THE FIRST WORD

A child's first word is a major milestone in her development, and an exciting event for everyone in her life. Yet while it might seem that starting to speak marks the beginning of language development, this is far from the truth. A baby's journey into language starts much earlier, going back to even before she is born. Infants only a few days old not only prefer their mother's voice over other voices, but they also show a distinct preference for their maternal language versus other languages, even when the voice of the speaker is unfamiliar. This suggests that while they are still in the womb, infants already start to tune into the rhythm and sounds of their mother tongue.

Fine-tuning of this process continues over the course of the first year of life, which is when babies start to figure out what contrasts matter in the language(s) they are acquiring. In fact, it turns out that young infants are much better than older children and adults at discriminating between a wide variety of speech sounds. In a series of studies, Janet Werker and her colleagues presented infants from English-speaking homes with sounds that contrast in the language they are exposed to, such as [ba] versus [da] in English, as well as sounds that contrast in another language, but not in English (e.g. [ta] vs [ʈa], two different 't' sounds in Hindi). In these experiments, infants were initially taught to turn their head towards a loudspeaker whenever the sound changed. The researchers then played the *ba/da* sounds, as well as the *ta/ʈa* sounds, and noted whether the infants turned their heads when [ba] changed to [da] (and vice versa), and when [ta] changed to [ʈa]. They found that while everyone was able to discriminate between [ba] and [da], only Hindi-speaking adults and 6- to 8-month-old babies (exposed only to English) were able to perceive the contrast between [ta] and [ʈa]. Strikingly, infants at the age of 10 to 12 months performed just as poorly as their English-speaking parents on this unfamiliar contrast. This suggests that by the end of the first year of life, before most children have said a single word, they have homed in on the sound system of the language(s) they are acquiring. (Werker and colleagues have published several studies. For an example, see Werker and Tees, 1984.)

The ability to perceive relevant sound contrasts is a critical skill for tackling what is perhaps one of the hardest problems in language learning overall: how to find words in fluent speech. Words are easy to identify on a written page, where they are flagged conveniently by blank space on either side. Yet no such blank space exists between words in spoken language. (If you are not convinced, find a radio station with a language you do not know, and try to identify words in the speech you are hearing.) So how do babies solve the task of what is called 'speech segmentation'? It seems that they use a variety of different cues. Language-specific stress patterns are one of them. For example, English nouns often consist of a stressed followed by an unstressed syllable (*DOggie, BAby*). Babies as young as 9 months of age seem to prefer stress patterns consistent with the language(s) they are learning, indicating that they are sensitive to the overall sound shape of words in their mother tongue(s).

Another dazzling skill that infants bring to the task of language learning is the ability to compute statistics over combinations of sounds. In other words, they seem to be able to keep track of which sounds occur together consistently, and are therefore likely to constitute a word. This was demonstrated in a set of experiments by Jenny Saffran and her colleagues, who had 8-month-old infants listen to two minutes of synthesized nonsense speech that sounded something like this: *bidakupadotigolabubida* . . . (Saffran et al., 1996). The sequence of sounds was carefully constructed such that some syllables always occurred next to each other (e.g. *bi* was always followed by *da*), whereas others did not (e.g. *ku* was followed by *pa* only a third of the time). Afterwards, infants were presented with 'words', that is, combinations of syllables that consistently occurred together, and 'non-words', which contained the same syllables, but in a different order from how they were encountered in the speech stream. Amazingly, babies listened longer to the unfamiliar combinations, suggesting that they were surprised by their novelty. This could only happen if they had somehow remembered what occurs next to what, that is, if they had kept track of co-occurrence statistics in the input they experienced.

If babies are naturally sophisticated speech perceivers and statistical analyzers, what role, if any, do parents and caregivers play in all this? Do babies just do it all on their own, or do they still need support from their environment? Some have argued that the special kind of baby talk, called 'motherese' or more neutrally **child-directed speech (CDS)**, that many of us adopt when we interact with an infant is critical for early language learning. CDS is characterized by exaggerated intonation, slower speech rate, short and often repetitive utterances and generally positive affect (see Chapter 6). Babies prefer to listen to child-directed compared to more adult-oriented speech. Yet while it seems that interactions involving CDS are enjoyable and of social and emotional relevance, it remains questionable whether CDS is in fact *necessary* for language acquisition to take place. One reason to be sceptical is that there is great variability across cultures regarding the extent to which speakers engage in CDS, and some have claimed that it does not exist at all in certain cultures. Nevertheless, children across the world acquire language and reach major milestones on a remarkably similar timescale. Moreover, no study has been able to show that increased exposure to CDS enhances or accelerates language development in any way. Does this mean we should give it up? Certainly not. CDS clearly contributes, among many other things, towards a rich, nurturing and interactive environment, which is exactly what babies need to thrive – physically, emotionally and linguistically.

A striking example of the importance of social interaction for early language learning comes from a study by Patricia Kuhl and her colleagues (Kuhl et al., 2003). They conducted an experiment similar to the ta/ʈa study described earlier, except that they looked at a different contrast, present in Mandarin Chinese but not in English ([ɕ] vs [tɕʰ]). American 10- to 12-month-olds exposed only to English were not able to discriminate between the two, just as one might expect. The researchers then provided another group of American infants with one of three types of exposure to Mandarin over a four-week period preceding the same discrimination experiment. The 'audio-only' group just listened to Mandarin speech without any visual cues, the 'audio-visual' group watched and listened to people interact in Mandarin on a television screen, while the 'live-interaction' group interacted with native Mandarin speakers in active play sessions. On the discrimination experiment, the first two groups performed just like the American babies who were never exposed to Mandarin. In other words, they were not able to detect the contrast. The 'live-interaction' group, however, was able to discriminate the contrast as well as babies from Mandarin-speaking homes. If acoustic perception and statistical computation were all it takes to learn a language, all three groups should have done equally well. Instead, these findings confirm what parents and caregivers instinctively know: It takes real humans and meaningful social interaction for all the innate dispositions a baby brings to the task of language learning to come to full fruition.

In sum, during the first year of life, babies are keen listeners and observers of the world and sounds around them. Driven by an innate predisposition for the task at hand, they extract a dazzling amount of information about the language(s) they experience around them, and they do so particularly through meaningful social interactions with the people in their lives.

TAKING OFF: WORDS AND BEYOND

In considering all the linguistic groundwork that infants engage in before they utter their first word, we have so far neglected one of the most important properties of words, namely that they connect strings of sounds with *meaning* (see Chapter 1). What exactly 'meaning' means has been a matter of debate among linguists and philosophers for several thousand years. In very general terms, learning the meaning of a word can be characterized as establishing a relationship between a string of sounds and an object, action, routine or concept observed, directly or indirectly, in the world. This is perhaps most straightforward in the case of concrete objects: You can point to your shoe and say *shoe*, thus providing the child with a linguistic label for a real-world object. Not surprisingly, children's early productive vocabularies consist primarily of such concrete nouns, along with words and phrases associated with social routines they frequently encounter in their lives (*bye, hi*).

Yet even with concrete objects which can be labelled ostensively, the learning task is not as straightforward as it might look. When I point to my shoe and say *shoe*, how do you know that I mean the entire shoe and not just the heel? How do you know that I am using my shoe as an example of footwear of this type more generally, rather than telling you the name of this specific shoe? The questions could go on and on, but it seems that children do not generally get sidetracked by possibilities like these. They tend to assume that a new word refers to a whole object, and that it refers to a type of thing, rather than a particular individual. These word learning strategies, called the 'Whole Object Assumption' and the 'Type Assumption', seem to guide children's word learning universally, and it has been suggested that they are part of our innate predisposition for learning language.

At the same time, word learning has an essentially social component. This has been demonstrated in experiments like the following, where 2-year-olds were presented with two stuffed toys they had never seen before (Moore et al., 1999). The experimenter looked at one of them and said *Look, there's Dodo!* At the very same time, the child's attention was drawn to the other toy by having it light up and move. Children were then asked to find *Dodo* to see whether they connected the word *Dodo* with the toy that was most salient (the one that lit up) or the one that was the object of their joint attention as indicated by the adult's eye gaze. They consistently picked up the latter, indicating that social interactive cues like shared eye gaze play an important role in language learning.

The fact that children seem to come to the task of word learning with the right strategies and sensitivity to social cues does not mean that they always nail it right away. Children often use words with meanings that are too narrow or too broad in terms of their adult definitions. For example, a child might use *shoe* only to refer to her own, baby-sized footwear, and not to her mother's kitten heels (which, admittedly, look quite distinct). This is known as **underextension** of a word's meaning. The converse, **overextension**, is also quite common: A child might use *shoe* not only to refer to footwear, but also to items used to cover hands (typically called *gloves* or *mittens* in English).

This does not indicate that the child is confused or does not understand the difference between feet and hands, but simply that she has not yet learned that English has a different label for hand wear as opposed to footwear (incidentally, a distinction that is not universal: In German, gloves are called *Handschuhe*, which literally means 'hand-shoes').

These early 'errors' in word learning illustrate a fundamental characteristic of language learning more generally: Children are creative and do not simply imitate what they hear from adults. The child might never have heard anyone label a glove, but she drew on her existing knowledge and generalized as best she could. The ability to generalize and to construct abstract rules becomes even more evident when we look at how children deal with linguistic material beyond nouns and verbs, namely functional items like the plural marker /-s/ in English. An English-speaking child might talk about her two *foots*, even though she almost certainly never heard her parents say this. If corrected, she might even be quite resistant to accepting that it should be *two feet*. Errors like these are called errors of **overgeneralization**, and are a sign of healthy development. They demonstrate that, contrary to popular belief, imitation only plays a limited role in language learning. In fact, studies have shown that it is quite rare to find a child immediately imitating or repeating an utterance addressed to her by an adult. Instead, children abstract over what they hear to build up the two critical components of linguistic competence: a 'mental lexicon' – a repository of word forms and meanings – and a 'grammar' – a system of abstract, unconscious rules and constraints that allows for the principled combination of words into a potentially infinite number of larger phrases and sentences. (See Chapter 2 for more information.)

Evidence of 'grammar' in its simplest form is present from children's very first multiword utterances. If we look at the word order in these early utterances, we see that it overwhelmingly matches the word order of the language the child is exposed to: Children learning English will say *eat cookie* (rather than *cookie eat*), reflecting that Objects follow Verbs in English. A child learning Japanese, by contrast, will almost certainly say *kukkii-(o) taberu* (literally: 'cookie eat'), consistent with the fact that Objects come before Verbs in Japanese. Beyond word order, an important part of learning the grammar of a language consists of learning small function words and inflection, such as the *-o* in *kukkii-o taberu* (a case marker, signalling that *kukkii* is the Object of the Verb). It is precisely this kind of material that tends to be missing during the telegraphic stage discussed earlier. Interestingly, some of these function words (like the English article *the*) are among the most frequent words in the language. Yet they tend to get omitted in children's speech for quite a long time, indicating that frequency of occurrence alone is also not what determines the course of development. In a classic study, Brown (1973) looked at 14 grammatical morphemes in the speech of three children learning English. He observed that all three children started using these morphemes appropriately in almost exactly the same order. When he looked at the frequency of these morphemes in the speech of their parents, he found that frequency of occurrence was not related to the order in which children started producing them. Instead, a number of linguistic factors, including phonological salience and grammatical complexity, were found to be more indicative of the order in which children acquire grammatical function words and inflection.

How exactly children ultimately arrive at the highly complex knowledge that characterizes adult linguistic competence, and within a highly constrained timeframe no less, still remains a mystery in many ways. Some hold that it can only be explained if we assume that a large portion of this abstract knowledge is innate. This proposal is generally associated with the modern-day linguist Noam Chomsky, but it dates back at least to the Classical Greek philosopher Plato. Others argue that information from the environment, together with general learning mechanisms to extract this information, is sufficient, and that postulating innate linguistic knowledge is unnecessary. The debate is unlikely to be resolved any time soon, but in its function of spurring scientific inquiry, it continues to contribute towards the assembly of more and more pieces in the millennia-old puzzle of how human babies come to acquire language.

LEARNING A NEW LANGUAGE AFTER CHILDHOOD

Everything we have said about language learning so far was based on children who were exposed to the language(s) they were learning from birth or very early childhood. Yet we all know, and most of us have experienced it, that languages can also be learned later in life. How is later, or **second language acquisition** (SLA) similar to or different from what we have said so far about **first language acquisition**? Perhaps the most striking difference that comes to mind is that second language (L2) learners rarely reach the same proficiency as native speakers. At first sight, this seems paradoxical: Why are little babies so much better at language learning than adults, who are generally far superior at learning other complex skills?

Some have argued that there is a biologically determined window of opportunity, a **critical period**, for language learning, similar to what has been observed in the animal world, where research has shown that songbirds must be exposed to the song of their species during a clearly specified time in their early lives, or they will never learn it (Lenneberg, 1967). Yet while biological maturation and neural commitment in the brain is likely to play a role, the case of L2 acquisition is different from the songbird scenario it is often compared to in a number of ways. Most importantly, L2 learners already have *a* language, their first language (L1). This provides them with a rich resource to draw on when learning an additional language, and with an immense head start compared to infants: A teenage exchange student immersed in an unfamiliar language environment for 12 months is highly likely to be more fluent than a 12-month-old infant raised in that environment. L2 learners draw on their L1 at just about every possible level, ranging from their knowledge of how a conversation between two speakers is typically structured, down to the grammatical structure of sentences. In cases where the two languages differ in any of these points, we tend to see the effects of **transfer**, that is, learners apply the structure of their L1 to their L2. For example, a French-speaking learner of English might say *She drinks often milk*, a sentence that sounds jarring to the native English speaker who would probably say *She often drinks milk*. The structure of French is such that adverbs like *often* must be placed after the verb. The learner's English sentence is reflective of this structure, indicating transfer at the level of syntactic structure.

If L2 learners begin by transferring everything they know about language from their L1, the starting point of L2 acquisition is a fundamentally different one from that in L1 acquisition. As a consequence, the learning trajectory – the path towards proficiency – must logically also be a different one. Nevertheless, research has shown remarkable similarities between L2 learners with very different mother tongues, suggesting that there are more general, L1-independent developmental patterns in L2 acquisition. For example, functional morphemes (like plural / s/ or the article *the*) are often missing in the speech of L2 learners, even those whose L1s have similar functional elements. This, of course, is reminiscent of the telegraphic stage in L1 development, and suggests that despite the many differences between L1 and L2 learning, both abide by what might be universal principles in language development. An important commonality between the two lies in the fact that a learner's developing L2, also called **interlanguage**, just like the child's developing L1, is a system governed by abstract rules, rather than based on imitation and correction alone. Our earlier example *She drinks often milk* is a good example: The learner is unlikely to have heard this from a native speaker, and might even have been corrected by a teacher at some point. Yet it seems that the abstract rules and constraints of her current interlanguage have overridden information from the L2 environment in this case.

This is not to say, however, that information from the environment and from interactions with other speakers do not play a role in L2 acquisition. In fact, differences in these domains might be an important contributor towards the differences we see in the outcomes of first versus later language acquisition. While infants are almost constantly immersed in the language around them, typically spoken by native speakers, many L2 learners experience their L2 only for limited periods of time in limited social settings (e.g. a classroom) and are often exposed to speech from other non-native speakers (e.g. their classmates). It is difficult to tease apart the effects of social factors like these from biological factors like brain maturation. It is highly likely that they contribute jointly to the development and outcomes we see in SLA. Like all human learning, language learning takes place at the crossroads of biology and social interaction. The many complex interactions that take place at this crossroads will remain a topic of research for many decades and centuries to come.

RELEVANCE TO EDUCATIONAL SETTINGS

We have seen that meaningful social interactions among real people provide the best possible environment for language learning, for children learning their first language(s) as much as for adults learning additional languages later in life. Classrooms can be such environments, regardless of whether the focus of instruction is on chemistry, music or early childhood education. Educators can create rich linguistic environments in their classrooms by enabling verbal interaction with and among students while pursuing the goals of the curriculum they teach. This will be of particular benefit to students whose access to the language of instruction is otherwise limited, for example, because they speak a different language at home, as is the case for many immigrant children.

We have also seen that despite the universal properties of human language development, there is great variability among learners as to when they reach major developmental milestones. Parents and educators should not expect all children to follow exactly the same time course. Variation within the limits we have discussed here is normal and should not be reason for concern. Yet if significant delays outside the normal range are suspected, it is important to consult professionals (paediatricians, clinical psychologists, audiologists, speech-language pathologists) for proper evaluation of a child's strengths and weaknesses. In any such evaluation, a child's social and family background should be taken into consideration. This is particularly important in the case of children who experience more than one language on a regular basis. If a language delay is suspected in a bilingual child, it is critical to understand to what extent this might be reflective of the child's limited experience with the language, or whether it potentially indicates a clinical condition.

DISCUSSION AND REFLECTION QUESTIONS

1   This chapter has shown that language learning involves both social and biological factors. In your opinion, what is the single most convincing piece of evidence that social factors are involved in language acquisition? What is the single most convincing piece of evidence that biological factors are involved in language acquisition?

2   If you see that a bilingual child in your classroom is having more trouble with the language of instruction than other children, does this indicate that this child might have SLI? What kind of information about the child could help you – and a speech-language pathologist – figure this out?

3   At the end of the chapter, it is suggested that teachers should create 'rich linguistic environments' in their classrooms, regardless of what subjects they teach. Can you think of some concrete things a teacher could do to create a 'rich linguistic environment' for the students in his or her classroom?

RECOMMENDED READING AND VIEWING

For a very readable and engaging introduction to child language acquisition from a linguistic perspective, accessible to anyone with an interest in the topic, see:
O'Grady, W. (2005), *How Children Learn Language*. Cambridge: Cambridge University Press.

For a comprehensive overview of language development from a multidisciplinary perspective, see:
Berko Gleason, J. and Bernstein Ratner, N. (2012), *The Development of Language* (8th edn). London: Allyn & Bacon.

For a research-based guide to bilingual development in children with and without language disorders, specifically written for parents, educators and clinicians, see:
Paradis, J., Genesee, F. and Crago, M. (2011), *Dual Language Development and Disorders* (2nd edn). Baltimore, MD: Paul H. Brookes.

For a thought-provoking documentary on language acquisition with interviews of major researchers in the field, see:

Searchinger, G. (1995), *The Human Language Series: Acquiring the Human Language* (part 2) [documentary]. New York: Equinox Films/Ways of Knowing Inc.

For an inspiring ten-minute talk about language learning in infancy, see Patricia Kuhl's TED talk on *The Linguistic Genius of Babies*:

www.ted.com/talks/patricia_kuhl_the_linguistic_genius_of_babies.html

6

How Do Speaking and Writing Support Each Other?

Christine C. M. Goh and
Paul Grahame Doyle

INTRODUCTION

Have you ever wondered about the differences between spoken and written language? Do people write the same way as they speak, or vice versa? When children go to school, they learn to read and write, but how do they continue to strengthen their ability to use spoken language? Does using the spoken language influence the development of their writing? These are just some questions that educators ask about the relationships between spoken and written language. In this chapter we will answer these questions by looking at the way spoken and written language support each other in a person's language development and language use.

We start with a comparison of the functions and features of speech and writing, and discuss the reciprocal relationship between the two. These ideas are then illustrated in a description of young children's ability to speak and write, highlighting the influence that family practices have on children's oracy and literacy development. This is followed by a discussion of the use of spoken and written language by children in school and the role of teachers' oral communication in class in their development of disciplinary literacies.

The term **oracy** will be used to refer to a person's ability to use the skills of speaking and listening in order to communicate and influence the social world they are in, including using talk to learn and construct knowledge jointly with others in both formal and informal contexts, while **literacy** refers to the development of reading and writing skills in both informal and academic contexts. The term 'literacy' also includes the broader notion of writing as social practice and **disciplinary literacy**. Moje (2008) has explained that literacy is not only what we read and write but also the ways of thinking and meaning which are appropriate to various subject disciplines.

FEATURES OF SPEECH AND WRITING

Humans have a need to relate to others, to share knowledge and information with one another and to pursue personal goals in social, emotional and physical realms. In fulfilling these needs, we use language as well as non-verbal elements to communicate a range of meanings and feelings. The ability and the need to communicate start from the moment a child is born. From their loud bawls to soft gurgles, babies communicate in various ways (see Chapter 5), including nascent gestures and facial expressions. Yet the most important form of communication as we grow older is through the use of language, both spoken and written.

Both written and spoken language can address the same topics and draw on many similar linguistic resources such as grammar and vocabulary. These are essentially resources for transmitting different kinds of meanings. The meaning might differ according to who the message is directed at and the purpose it serves. For example, an invitation to friends to have dinner together could take the form of a simple phone call or a text message, but an invitation to a special guest at a formal dinner would typically be made through writing a formal letter or email. In the first type of invitation, the meaning conveyed is one of coming together for good food and company, while the second type of invitation is a formal request for someone special or important to attend an event (see also Chapter 3). Spoken and written communications not only serve different social functions, but they also have their own unique features:

- First, spoken language is typically produced spontaneously and constructed together by partners in an interaction. What someone says is often influenced by what another person has said or might be expected to say. The meaning communicated is also negotiated for clarity through strategies such as asking for repetition or paraphrasing. Written language, on the other hand, is typically planned by a single writer for a distant reader but may undergo several rounds of drafting so that the reader will understand the meaning clearly and the communication purpose is achieved.

- Secondly, spoken language is mainly produced in face-to-face interactions in which the speaker can refer to the objects, people, places, etc. that are in the context of interaction without explicitly mentioning them. Written language, on the other hand, is used when the writer and the reader are separated by space and time; the writer, therefore, has to convey thoughts and information in a linguistically explicit manner.

- Thirdly, compared with written language, natural speech tends to be 'messy': Not all sentences are well formed and there are redundancies, repetitions and hesitations. Content communicated through writing is relatively compact, with information embedded in well-constructed sentences.

- Fourthly, spoken and written language are different in terms of **lexical density** (Halliday, 1989). This means there is a difference in the ratio of 'content words', such as nouns (e.g. *house, happiness, May*), verbs (e.g. *return, like, play*), adjectives (e.g. *red, patient, important*) and adverbs (e.g. *slowly, candidly, later*) to 'function words', such as articles (e.g. *a, an, the*), prepositions (e.g. *over, in, above*) and conjunctions (e.g. *and, but, when*) in relation to the length of the clause or sentence. Written language tends to pack more content words into a sentence or clause compared with spoken language. Look at Examples 1 and 2:

Example 1. Written language

Drawing on a *substantial research base*, the *book examines* the *process* of *child language acquisition* and *development*. (Total – 17 words: Content words (italics) – 11, function words – 6)

Example 2. Spoken language

This *book draws* on a *large number* of *studies* to *examine* the *ways* in which *children acquire* and *develop* a *language*. (Total – 21 words: Content words (italics) – 11, function words – 10)

Structurally, there are also differences between speech and writing. In speech, for example, clauses are linked by simple conjunctions such as *and, but, so,* compared with writing, where there might be more embedding of clauses within a complex sentence. This is because speech is produced in real time when speakers often might not have the cognitive capacity to construct very elaborate sentences while monitoring what they are saying. Speech which tends to be highly contextualized also contains many **ellipses**, that is to say words or phrases are left out because the meaning is already clear from the context. For example, instead of asking someone in your family *Would you like a cup of coffee?* you might say *Coffee?* Spoken language also contains many **deictic items**, such as *this*, *that*, *there* and various pronouns which are used to point to objects, people, places, etc. in a context of interaction.

Although spoken and written language may occur in very specific contexts, there are some contexts where the language produced has features of both speech and writing, thus blurring the distinction between the two. News and weather reports are two such examples. The proliferation of information communication technologies has also created new contexts which merge speech and writing in everyday communication through online chats, social media messages, emails and texting. In other words, it is possible to have speech which is planned and rehearsed, as well as written language which is unplanned and more spontaneous like speech and which includes features of spoken grammar such as ellipsis. Technological changes notwithstanding, there are some contexts in which spoken language is used more frequently, such as in face-to-face social interactions, business meetings, and teaching and learning in schools. Written language, on the other hand, is the preferred mode where permanence is essential. For example, the transience of discussions conducted orally at a meeting is often captured in the form of meeting minutes for future action and reference. We can therefore think of language production 'as a kind of continuum, with "most spoken" texts that relate to immediate action at one end and "most written" texts that are abstract and reflective at the other' and somewhere in the middle of the continuum are texts which have characteristics of both modes (Goh and Burns, 2012, p. 79).

RELATIONSHIP BETWEEN SPEAKING AND WRITING

The relationship between speaking and writing has long been perceived to be mainly unidirectional with speech laying the foundation for writing. In other words, a child's development in writing depends on his or her knowledge of the spoken language to express meaning. The role of speech in supporting second language writing development has also been recognized (Weissberg, 2006). A reciprocal relationship between speaking and writing, however, has been proposed by Kantor and Rubin (1981). Writing, they claim, has been perceived as a more advanced code that develops out of speech. Whereas speech seems to require relatively less overt teaching, writing development requires instruction. In further explicating the relationship between speaking and writing, Rubin and Kang suggest that the oral-writing relationship is more like strands of DNA, saying, 'A more apt model might be a double helix with a writing strand and a speaking strand intertwined. At any particular stage one strand may be the focal outcome, drawing upon the other. But as a whole, the two strands are reciprocally supportive and leading in the same direction' (2008, p. 220). They give the examples of poster presentations and briefings as types of collaborative discourse in which the written word guides the formal talk. The model they posit finds support in a cognitive view of speech and language processing. Speakers have to conceptualize or select the content of the message, formulate utterances by using available linguistic resources and articulate the message for their listeners' comprehension (Levelt, 1989). Writing ideas down, whether as a draft of a speech or simply as an outline to remember, is a process of planning and rehearsal which can help free up a speakers' cognitive space and increase his or her capacity for articulation and monitoring of speech.

Pedagogical practice has enthusiastically embraced the role of speaking in writing development as shown in the 'using talk to support writing' approach for developing early writing (Fisher et al., 2010) and the 'talk for writing' approach to teaching creative writing (Corbett and Strong, 2011). These approaches have focused mainly on the language learners' own or collaborative talk and its influence on their writing. Lwin and Teo (2011), on the other hand, have proposed a method that uses the spoken output of more accomplished speakers to help less accomplished learners in their writing. They suggest that teachers guide learners in identifying transitional cues in the narratives of professional storytellers (e.g. specific ways of using verbal and non-verbal features to sustain an audience's interest as the storyline develops), and applying similar cues in the learners' own written narratives to achieve similar effects.

ACQUIRING SPOKEN AND WRITTEN LANGUAGE

When we acquire our first language, we develop the ability to communicate our needs and intentions through spoken language first, before learning to convey these and other meanings through writing. This ability of children and language learners to write about something that they are able to talk about entails not just richness of content and meaning but also command of language features and forms that are needed to express meanings in a clear and precise manner.

As children listen to the speech of others around them and directed at them, children learn that language is used to fulfill communicative goals. They gradually learn to use language to ask for things they need, express their preferences, explore how things work in their world, and interact through play and routines. They also learn to verbalize their private thoughts, as well as narrating events that they have experienced or stories that they have heard or created themselves. Their increasing facility with spoken language enables children to express a wide range of needs and intentions, comprehend meanings in other people's utterances, initiate an interaction by introducing, maintaining and closing a topic, show that they share the perspectives of the people they are talking with, and adapt what they have to say to what they think these people are thinking. To manage extended discourse, children resort to a variety of linguistic strategies such as using conjunctions (*and, then, and then, after that*) to connect different parts of a story and using adverbials of time (*One day, Once upon a time, The end*) to structure it clearly for the listeners. Children who have opportunities to develop the skills of reading and writing will use the written language to communicate all these and other more sophisticated meanings as their contexts of interaction and learning evolve in complexity.

Examples of a child learning to speak and write

Language acquisition experts tell us that most children will acquire their home language by the time they are 4 or 5 years old (see Chapter 5). They are normally able to speak and understand the language fairly accurately, thus enabling them to convey and interpret meanings in their immediate social contexts. It is also around this time that many children develop their abilities to read and write. Below are examples of spoken and written language produced by Nicole, a 4-year-old girl acquiring English as a first language. In Example 3, Nicole was relating something she had watched on television. In Example 4 she was explaining how to make a windmill after watching a short cartoon called *The Old Mill*.

Example 3

The elephant became flat, then he became real, then everybody chased him.

Example 4

First, make a triangle. Then make a square. Then make lots of things that go round. Then we take, we stick them all together. And then we take, we take, some, then we take, put another square. Then we have to put a triangle at the top. There, finished! It's a windmill. At the top are all the bats.

(Goh and Silver, 2006, pp. 173, 178)

In the above examples, Nicole demonstrated her ability to organize extended discourse by using the words *first* and *then* indicating chronological sequencing. She was also able to let her listeners know that she had come to the end of what she was saying with *There, finished!* In giving specific directions on how to assemble the various parts of the windmill, Nicole correctly used the imperative form *Make a triangle.* She also showed her command of vocabulary about shapes such as *flat*, *square* and *triangle* and action verbs, such as *make take, stick* and *put*. She used the declarative form correctly when stating something *The elephant became flat, It's a windmill, At the top are all the bats*. Nicole's acquisition of these linguistic features enabled her to organize an extended piece of discourse for her listeners' understanding. Example 5 is a short written narrative by Nicole at the same age.

Example 5

Nicole's narrative   **Comments**

Nicole wrote the title of her story *The Rat and the cat* on the page and drew a large frame around it. This special design shows that she was aware of the way a picture book was normally organized, starting with a cover page which showed the title of the book.

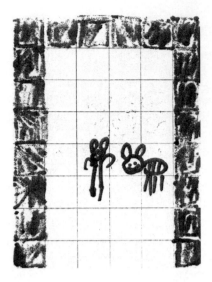

On the next page, Nicole drew a rat on the left and a cat on the right. No text was included. This resembled illustrations found in some inside pages of picture books that Nicole had read.

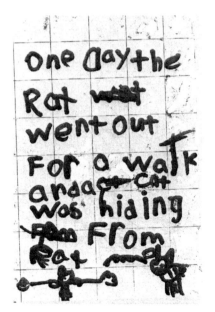

Nicole began her story on the third consecutive page with *one day the Rat went out for a walk and a cat was hiding From Rat*. There was a clear **orientation** or introduction to the characters, the time and the place where the event occurred. It was signaled by the phrase *One day*, a common expression found in children's stories, as well as the mention of the two main characters, the rat and the cat. (See Chapter 3 for more information about narrative structure.)

Note that Nicole had not learnt to use capitalization at the start of a sentence; there were also no punctuation marks in her story and some letters were not formed properly. Capital letters when used also appeared to be random. Nevertheless, Nicole was able to use the simple past and past continuous tense to express the action in relation to the context. Other than just writing her story, Nicole also included a drawing of a cat and a rat, producing a multimodal text. (See, again Chapter 3.)

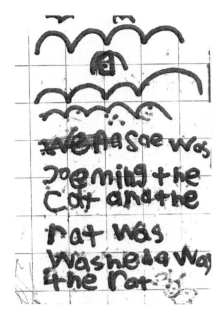

Nicole's multimodal output is further seen in the next page where she drew waves and what looked like an animal swept by the waves. Nicole's awareness of a narrative structure is evident as she introduced a **problem** (typically found in narratives as part of the plot development): *sae was ɔoeming the cat and the rat was washed a way*. Although the words *sea, coming* and *away* had not been spelt correctly, the meaning was intact. Once again, there were no punctuation marks such as full stops, but Nicole wrote her next sentence beginning with *The rat* as a new line, suggesting some conceptual understanding of setting a boundary between two idea units.

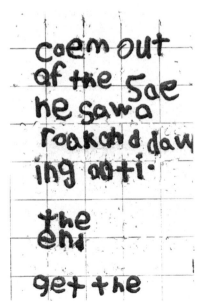

Next, Nicole provided a **resolution** to the problem, but the meaning of the last few words was not completely clear because of her handwriting and spelling. She continued the sentence from the previous page (*the rat* at the bottom of the previous page): *The rat coem out of the sae he saw a roak and claw ing on ti.* (Note the misspellings: *coem, sae, roak, ti.*) Interestingly, there seems to be a full stop at the end of the last sentence. To end her story, Nicole also wrote the words *the end* and included a remark telling her 'reader' to get the next story. However, she only wrote two words *get the* and finished the rest of the sentence by saying *next story* aloud.

In the above narrative, we can see Nicole's command of various aspects of the English language such as syntax, morphology and vocabulary, as well as **pragmatic competence** in organizing her discourse. A comparison of her oral and written language shows that her writing reflects the spoken language she would have used if she were to tell the story aloud. For example, Nicole had already acquired the ability to use declarative statements in her speech, while the use of coordination was present in many samples of her earlier speech (e.g. *It fell down and broke its head*). Two years later, in the first two months of primary school, Nicole wrote sentences which combined clauses to express meanings with greater precision in a more complex and formal piece of writing (Example 6).

Example 6

Primary 1.3

My Ambition

when I grow up I want dentist because I wan hlep little children take care of their teeth uder wise, Ciildren Would have Black teeth and their teeth would fall out and they cant eat hard food like carrots and bisciutes. as rewards

On the special worksheet given by her teacher, Nicole wrote the title of her composition *My Ambition* and her text: *when I grow up I want dentist, because I want hlep little children, take care of their teeth uder wise, Children Would have Black teeth, and their teeth would fall out and, they cant eat hard food like, carrots and bisciutes as rewards*. The complexity in Nicole's spoken language was evident in this piece of written work. She used a subordinate clause *When I grow up* and expressed conditions using both the modal verb *would* and the adverb *otherwise*. Clauses were also coordinated with the conjunction *and*, a key feature of spoken grammar. Although she had not learnt to use capitalization and punctuation accurately, Nicole inserted a comma to indicate a pause whenever she ran out of space at the end of every line. The apostrophe in *can't* was missing and no full stops were used.

Learning to convey their meaning through the written word can be challenging for children. In developing their literacy skills, children have to master the symbols that represent their written language. In acquiring writing skills in English, for example, children have to learn the letters in the English alphabet and learn how the sound or sounds of each letter are the same or not the same as the sounds they hear in everyday interaction and which they themselves are already articulating. They also need to learn how the sounds in the letters blend to make the words that they speak and hear. The ability to spell as illustrated in the above example is an area that schools spend time developing with children.

Influence of home practices

Children acquire language through their interaction with adults such as parents and caregivers, and sometimes even peers. There is research evidence to show that much of children's oracy development (and subsequently literacy development) is influenced by rich language and literacy practices in the home (Hart and Risley, 1995). An example of this is the use of **contingent speech** by adults to respond to topics that a child introduces, thereby prolonging the conversation and allowing the child more opportunities to speak. Look at Example 7.

Example 7

Nicole: What is a monster?

Mother: A monster is a big creature. It's usually quite scary.

Nicole: I'm not scared.

Mother: No, you don't need to be scared. Monsters aren't real. You only find them in stories.

Nicole: Why are they found only in stories?

Mother: Because people put them there to scare little children and make their stories exciting.

The utterances produced by the adult above are referred to as contingent utterances because they are dependent on what the child says first. Contingent utterances can encourage children to develop their spoken language and thinking because of the **scaffolding** or structured help that adults provide through extending the conversation. Through scaffolding children's talk, adults help children to accomplish a task (in this case engaging in a conversation) which the children would otherwise not be able to achieve on their own. Scaffolding through contingent utterances is an important part of children's language development process. On the other hand, if adults use speech mainly to control children's behaviour, they would not be providing the children with the help needed for developing more advanced speaking skills.

Children's early achievements in school are increasingly seen to be closely linked to the use of speech at home. Preschooler's oracy skills have been shown to be a good predictor of their early as well as later literacy in schools. When preschool children are exposed to ways of using speech that enable better thinking and expression of ideas, they are in fact learning to develop ways of using language that are valued in 'formal' education which they will soon be a part of. Snow and associates have long researched the use of abstract language, or what they refer to as **decontextualized oral language**, and how the use of such language can positively influence literacy skills and academic success when children enter schools (e.g. Snow et al., 1995). Decontextualized oral language skills refer to 'the ability to talk about that which is beyond the immediate context' (p. 38).

Example 7 showed that contingent speech can lead to decontextualized oral language use when the conversation focuses on ideas that are abstract and beyond what is seen in the face-to-face interaction context for mother and child. Contingent speech can also help children learn the importance of providing explanations and details in what they say, as Example 8 shows.

Example 8

Nicole: When I was making this, I was deciding to make a rocket.

Mother: Why didn't you make it then?

Nicole: Because it's too dangerous

Parents also teach preschool children language and concepts through talk, as can be seen in Example 9 where the adult confirmed what the child had said and introduced the word *thought* to represent the experience that the child felt. The use of the abstract noun *thought* not only repeats and affirms Nicole's original meaning, it also exposes her to the concept of **nominalization**, a feature of advanced literacy which she will encounter frequently in school.

Example 9

Nicole: I don't need to open my mouth. I just close my mouth and I can hear what I say in my heart.

Mother: Yes, that's your *thought*.

In Example 10, Nicole's father introduced the word *skeletons* to help her express her idea more precisely.

Example 10

Nicole: Does a spider have X-ray?

Father: X-ray? No.

Nicole: Then it'll be a puddle of mud.

Father: You mean *skeletons*, don't you?

Nicole: Hmm (nods)

Frequent engagement in this type of abstract or decontexualized talk at home can prepare children to engage in similar types of talk and thinking in school. As they participate in formal education, they will build on this ability to be precise and accurate and will further develop their ability to express their ideas and thinking in both speech and writing. Children who have been socialized into this way of talking and thinking have a distinct advantage in school (Dickinson and Tabors, 2001).

DEVELOPING ADVANCED AND DISCIPLINARY LITERACIES

Children continue to use speech to fulfill an ever increasing range of social functions when they are in primary and secondary school. Primary school children improve their conversation skills by learning to manage the topic and close a conversation less abruptly, as well as by using better turn taking strategies during a conversation. They also develop new ways of manipulating language in ways which they think are acceptable to their peers, teachers or other adults. For example, children learn to explain reasons for their behaviour so as to be excused for their actions. They also learn to be more indirect in their use of language, for example, when making a request or asking for something. They develop more mature forms of narrative which have more complex plots compared to the simple narratives produced in preschool years. This is also the time when children encounter academic language for explaining, defining and illustrating concepts they learn in the school curriculum.

They also more frequently encounter written texts of greater length. As they encounter more written language in their school text books and other learning materials, children develop their reading and writing abilities helped by a strong foundation in oral language use and emergent literacy in preschool years. They continue to learn penmanship, that is, the ability to hold writing implements such as pencils and form letters and words on paper. In this age of advanced communication technology, many children also need to acquire the ability to comprehend and produce written texts in electronic forms.

Secondary school students develop explicit knowledge about language and language use. They use language creatively for jokes and become more aware of shades of meanings in words. They also continue to develop greater facility with using speech for academic purposes such as in discussions and debates. At the same time, they develop more advanced forms of literacy which enable them to participate in academic learning through engaging with the written language in print and online media. The sentences they encounter and produce in primary school are syntactically simple, but in secondary schools students learn to use more complex sentence structures that are less similar to the grammar of speech. Christie (2002) observed that secondary school children develop a feature of advanced literacy known as **nominalization**. This is a process by which a clause with a main verb (or other parts of speech such as adjective) is changed to a noun group, giving the written text a more abstract and formal nature compared with speech. In Example 11, the verb *saw* has been turned into a noun *sight*. By doing this, the writer is no longer describing an action, a common feature of speech, but shifts the attention to a phenomenon or concept.

Example 11

Tim saw his mother crying in the room. He felt sad.

The sight of his mother crying in the room made Tim sad.

From learning to write simple sentences and compose narratives, older children develop a greater awareness of the value that is ascribed to the written language in school learning as they continue to learn about the difference between the purpose and nature of the use of speech and writing in their daily communication (see also Chapter 3). They also read and produce texts for various subjects, thereby learning how to understand and use the grammar of written English differently from their experience in primary schools (Christie, 2002).

Similar to parents' and caregivers' use of contingent speech at home, teachers' use of contingent responses can provide opportunities for the use of language that is characteristic of the thinking processes associated with being literate: explicitness, connectivity, justification and relevance. Students' encounter with language in school, particularly in the classroom, provides them with new opportunities to develop not only their general oracy and literacy abilities but also ways of speaking, listening, reading and writing that are appropriate for the various subject disciplines in the school curriculum.

Just as young children are socialized in ways of thinking and acting through conversations with adults, children in school can learn ways of making meaning and behaving through oral interactions with teachers and their peers in class. For example, a history teacher can use questions not merely to elicit facts but to encourage learners to develop a way of thinking that is appropriate for students of history, such as evaluating the sources of information. Recently, the notion of **disciplinary literacy** (Moje, 2008; Shanahan and Shanahan, 2008) has gained ground with educators as a way of explaining the gap between student achievement and the demands of employers and institutes of higher learning recognized in many developed economies. The recognition that many students, whether their first language is English or not, cannot navigate successfully between the literacies of their everyday lives and those required in studying school subjects, has led to investigation of how disciplines are represented in school subject teaching.

The notion of literate thinking through oracy is consistent with current conceptions and understanding of literacy. Students need to develop at least two kinds of oracy skills for academic learning: presentational talk and exploratory talk (see Chapter 7). Presentational talk has characteristics that are closer to the 'more written' type of spoken language which we highlighted earlier. It normally requires planning how to select the language and organize the discourse so that ideas are conveyed to a formal audience only after some amount of redrafting and rehearsal by the speaker. Some examples of presentational talk are project presentations, show and tell, and to some extent, formal debate. Exploratory talk, on the other hand, is spontaneous and less structured. It happens mainly during group discussions where students engage with one another's ideas. They do not merely agree all the time but take on the roles to develop and critique ideas, challenging ideas from peers and giving reasons when they agree or disagree with one another. The aim is to arrive at a better understanding of the matter at hand through thinking together or 'interthinking' (Mercer, 2000).

The essential idea of exploratory talk is that learners come to a new topic or new concept with their existing language resources, and use these resources to try to establish meaning through discussion prompted by the teacher. In essence, this is also the heart of inquiry-based learning: The teacher uses a pedagogical framework that will prompt students to engage in focused discussion around a key aspect of the subject syllabus, for example, *heat* or *the divine right of Kings* or *polynomial expressions.* In order to develop disciplinary literacy, students need to progress to using talk that adopts the structures and vocabulary of the academic discipline (Resnick et al., 2010). How this transition can be managed has so far received little attention by researchers. Yet creating classroom opportunities for this type of talk holds promise for subject teachers interested in helping their students' to write more precisely and cogently, and to demonstrate understanding and application of key concepts and theories for their subject.

The teacher's role, therefore, is more than one of prompting discussion, as is the case with exploratory talk. Now, scaffolding the process of inquiry and modelling the appropriate subject specific language are critical aspects of a pedagogic transition from exploratory talk to talk that aligns more closely with the way scientists or historians or mathematicians might talk about their typical problems. This gradual acculturation of the student's ways of thinking and communicating into subject literacy (Moje, 2008) prepares the student for developing a disciplinary 'voice'. Without this preparation, that voice will not exist, will not be heard or will not be recognized. The writer cannot emerge until the voice is found and has gained timbre from rehearsing the genres in oral interactions with peers and knowledgeable others (teachers). Students cannot talk and write like scientists because they have not entered into the **discourse community** of science; they have yet to navigate the literacies of school as opposed to those of everyday life in their communities (Moje et al., 2008). They will continue to develop these voices in speech and writing throughout their school years, and into tertiary education if they enter college. As Wells (1992, p. 291) observed, learning the discourses in school is not unlike the conversational learning of children in their preschool years and 'can be seen quite largely as a continuing apprenticeship in discourse, as he or she participates in, and takes over, the different discourse genres – that is, ways of making meaning – that are encountered in various subjects of the curriculum'. Throughout this process of apprenticeship, children and adolescents will continue to develop their knowledge and skill in speaking and writing. This reciprocal relationship between speaking and writing is essential for the development of disciplinary literacy.

RELEVANCE TO EDUCATIONAL SETTINGS

Oracy and literacy are both important competencies that children need to develop from a young age. The foundation that is laid in preschool and primary school years will enable them to develop more advanced forms of language use to achieve myriad purposes in secondary and tertiary contexts. These abilities are just as important for those who join the workforce after their school education. Based on the preceding discussion of the relationship between speaking and writing, we would like to suggest some considerations for teachers.

Be aware of the different language backgrounds that your students come from. While there are obvious differences in home languages, such as English, Chinese or Spanish, there are also qualitative differences in the way language is used for thinking among families speaking the same language. When children come from homes where there is less use of language for abstract thinking and learning, these children might be at a disadvantage as they have not yet learnt to acquire the knowledge and the types of talk and thinking that is valued and promoted in educational settings. If these children also come from homes that do not speak the language of instruction, these children will be doubly disadvantaged when they begin formal education and are rushed into literacy in the school language (see Chapter 8). The role of the school, therefore, is to help these children develop their competencies in using language to listen, speak, read and write, as well as improving their ability to think individually and together with other children through these modalities of language use.

Given the reciprocal relationship between spoken and written language in the overall language development of children and other language learners, teachers need also to be aware of the opportunities there are for helping students develop oracy and literacy skills in an integrated manner. In situations where language learners may not have a well-developed verbal repertoire to support the thinking process in writing classes, teachers can also draw on linguistic and learning resources through reading. They should nevertheless continue to encourage language learners to develop greater facility with speaking and listening, as these are important avenues for acquiring a language which will ultimately have an impact on the development of more advanced forms of literacy.

Teachers should be familiar with the key features of speech and writing and recognize that language production is a continuum. They should also recognize that spoken and written language are often used for different purposes and would therefore need to help students recognize these features and purposes to direct their own learning and use of the language. For example, teachers should not expect students to produce the same kinds of sentences in both speaking and writing even though the topic may be the same. In fact, students should be taught how they should adjust their language production according to spoken and written modes by constructing utterances or sentences that take into account the difference between the two modes in terms of context and forms of interaction.

Teachers, particularly academic subject teachers, should be aware of the potential that spoken language during classroom teaching and interaction can have on academic learning. This means that teachers should develop a deep understanding of the role that language plays in mediating the content, of holding together the other modalities (visual and tactile) and symbolic languages (formulae and expressions), and of constructing the curriculum genre. Thus, in science, knowing that *poly-* means 'many' or 'multiple' and that *photo-* means 'light' is enabling. Children can only develop their abilities to manage the various genres of schooling with the help of their teachers who are experts in the thinking and the language use associated with their respective disciplines. In doing this, they will be facilitating their students' 'continuing apprenticeship in discourse' (Wells, 1992, p. 291) in spoken and written language valued by the communities of the different disciplines represented in the subjects in the school curriculum.

DISCUSSION AND REFLECTION QUESTIONS

1 Why do you think it is important for language teachers to understand the similarities and differences between spoken and written language? How would you use this knowledge to assist you in teaching your students about language production and language use?

2 Referring to the samples from the child's spoken and written English (Examples 3–10), discuss how children's conversational learning in preschool years might influence their written language. Do you think children whose home language is not English will be disadvantaged when learning to read and write in English?

3 How can teachers maximize opportunities for students to learn to acquire the various genres of schooling? What factors could influence students' development of disciplinary literacy at each stage of their schooling?

RECOMMENDED READING AND VIEWING

To read more on research and theoretical insights into the various ways in which second language speaking and writing support each other, see:
Belcher, D. and Hirvela, A. (eds) (2008), *The Oral-Literate Connection: Perspectives on L2 Speaking, Writing and Other Media Instructions*. Ann Arbor, MI: University of Michigan Press.

For an explanation of spoken grammar and authentic language samples that illustrate key features of spoken grammar, see:

Carter, R. and McCarthy, M. (1997), *Exploring Spoken English*. Cambridge: Cambridge University Press.

For an introduction to how children develop their oracy and literacy skills from preschool to secondary school years, see:

Goh, C. C. M. and Silver, R. E. (2006), *Language Learning: Home, School and Society*. Singapore: Pearson Longman.

To learn more about how social interaction and speaking play an important role in writing development and strategies that teachers can use in a writing class, see:

Weissberg, R. (2006), *Connecting Speaking & Writing in Second Language Writing Instruction*. Ann Arbor, MI: Michigan Series on Teaching Multilingual Writers.

For a lecture on disciplinary literacy by Professor Elizabeth Moje, see:
www.youtube.com/watch?v=ld4gKJ-wGzU

7

How Is Language Used for Learning?

Rita Elaine Silver, Raslinda A. R. and Galyna Kogut

INTRODUCTION

Chapter 1 of this book notes that language is pervasive in our lives. It is also pervasive in classes – language classes and classes for other academic subjects. However, language use in classes has some special features which are different to language use at home. In addition, while students are still developing and refining language proficiency and skills, they are also developing language for study of academic subjects. Thus, part of learning to be successful in school is learning how to use school language, or **academic language** as we usually call it. For example, referring to mathematics knowledge and English language learners (or, as they call them, Limited English Proficiency [LEP] students), Secada and Carey wrote more than 20 years ago that

> many teachers (and researchers) confound how people use mathematical language with actual knowledge of mathematics. People who sound like they know what they are talking about are judged to have knowledge,

while those who don't express themselves well are judged not to have such knowledge. However, if the best practices begin where students are academically, then teachers of LEP [Limited English Proficiency] students need to begin not only with what students understand but also with how they can express their understandings. Further, teachers should help students develop both mathematical understanding and its communication. (1990, p. 3)

This is still something teachers need to be aware of – for every subject they teach. Therefore, this chapter deals explicitly with language in educational contexts and in particular with classroom talk. This is because most classroom lessons rely on talk for teaching and learning. Ideas that we are trying to teach are introduced through talk and language itself is often taught through classroom talk. This chapter introduces how language is used to study across academic subjects. The focus then moves explicitly to the different ways teachers can use talk in the classroom, including pros and cons of different types of teacher talk. Student talk is equally important; we include discussion of peer talk and of different types of student talk.

As you read, you will see several excerpts from transcripts of classroom talk. These are examples to help you see classroom talk in action. All of these excerpts are taken from middle primary grade classrooms in Singapore – a context in which students from different home languages study English language and use English as the medium of instruction. We hope that by providing excerpts from one context and similar grade levels, the examples will be more easily comparable. Information on how to read the transcripts is included along with our interpretations.

LANGUAGE USE IN ACADEMIC STUDY

Here is a problem of the type often used in primary school mathematics textbooks:

> If Xin Hui has 10 apples and Rachel has 2 more than Xin Hui, how many apples does Rachel have?

To solve the problem, children need to use simple addition (10 + 2 = 12), so the mathematical concept is not very difficult. What people might not notice is that in addition to basic mathematics skills, children must be able to understand the *language* in the problem. They must, for example, identify that Xin Hui and Rachel are people in order to interpret the situation – which might be more or less difficult depending on their knowledge of names from different languages and cultures. More difficult is understanding the grammatical structure with *more than* and *if*. A more straightforward way to phrase the same problem is:

> *Xin Hui has 10 apples. Rachel has 2 more apples than Xin Hui. How many apples does Rachel have?*

Learning to understand and use comparatives such as *more/less than* is an important part of mathematic concept building, but it is also a language issue, especially when combined with hypothetical phrases such as *if*. The difficulty for a teacher is to ascertain whether a child is lacking the necessary mathematical knowledge or language knowledge to sort out the problem statement.

Because of these different language requirements across academic subjects (e.g. mathematics, biology, economics, health, geography) studying in these topics can also help to develop advanced language and literacy skills. In other words, as students work with the different language and literacy requirements in the context of academic subjects, they have the opportunity to learn more language and develop literacy skills through contextualized use. In addition, study in the sciences and social sciences can provide purposeful contexts for extended writing; however, teachers need to be aware of the different language resources required for different types of writing in different academic subjects. Writing is also recommended for mathematics learning: As students are pushed to put their thinking into words, they also clarify their ideas. Whatever the academic subject, writing also encourages use of more complex grammatical structures required for description, explanation and persuasion. While Chapter 6 has addressed this with reference to the necessary disciplinary requirements of different academic subjects, it is useful to note that language study is also interdisciplinary. Some aspects of language cross academic boundaries, making language a crucial part of schooling in all subjects. In the next section, we talk about how language is used in classrooms for teaching and learning.

CLASSROOM TALK

Over time there have been many suggestions for organizing classrooms to incorporate more media and information technology, more peer and group work, and different types of learning and teaching strategies. Although there are many recommendations for ways of organizing learning, lessons are still dominated by teacher-fronted classroom interactions and inundated with teacher talk.

How do teachers use talk in classrooms?

Teacher talk is one of the components of classroom interaction, often the dominant component. The way teachers use language with students is important as the main purposes of schooling are achieved through communication. The way a teacher plans, carries out and controls classroom talk influences learning and the whole educational process. Let's look at an example of talk in a primary school classroom to see how this works. Excerpt 1 is taken from a longer transcript of a grade 4 mathematics lesson in Singapore. The medium of instruction is English. The students are doing calculations with money and learning to use graphs to chart calculations with different coins (i.e. 50 cent and 20 cent coins). The students have tried to do one problem independently. At the beginning of the excerpt the teacher is getting ready to check their answers.

First, a few words about how to read the transcript: Each turn is marked with a number on the left side of the transcript. The second column shows who is talking: the teacher, a student or many students. All of the names are pseudonyms. The third column shows what was said. Note that classroom talk is spontaneous and so there might be some pauses (marked by ' . . . ' in the excerpt), some false starts or 'incorrect' wording because that is the way people speak during spontaneous production. Additional information about actions (e.g. laughing, gesturing), use of classroom tools (e.g. showing images on the projector) are shown in parenthesis (_). These are intended to help you get a fuller picture of what was happening although transcripts, by necessity, always miss a lot of the non-verbal and gestural communication in a lesson. Finally, bear in mind that classroom talk is rarely as tidy as it looks in a transcript: There might be more than one person speaking, more than one conversation ongoing, interruptions or misunderstandings which require quite a bit of back and forth to resolve. The transcript excerpts shown in this chapter tend to show the dominant classroom conversation to illustrate specific points; they are not intended to represent everything going on in a classroom lesson at a specific point in time.

Excerpt 1 starts at turn 1 with the teacher talking to the class as a whole, finding out who has completed the problem and then moving on to check the students' work.

Excerpt 1 Learning about money (Mathematics lesson)

1	Teacher	Ok, how many of you have finished . . . How many of you with the answer? You may not be sure whether your answer is right. (Some hands go up.) Good. Hands down. How many of you are quite confident that your answer is correct? (Some hands go up.) Good. I like to see that kind of confidence. Put down your hand. If you follow the method that you have learnt and you are careful with your calculation your answers should be. How many of you found the number of 50 cent coins to be 2? (Some hands go up.)
2		(One student says something indistinct to the teacher. This could not be picked up from the recording equipment.)
3	Teacher	Good. Put down your hands. And how many of you found the number of 20 cents coins to be 8? (Some hands go up.)
4	Some students	8.
5	Teacher	Very good! Put down your hands. Ok, the next thing is we will have to make sure that your tabulation, the table that you draw, is correct. So do you have . . . Let me see. Where is a good sample to show? Ok, let's say this one. (The teacher takes one student's paper to use as an example. The teacher shows it on the class projector, pointing to it while talking.) 50 cents. Ok. Amount? Where is the amount?
6	Students	He he he he! (laughing) Amo! (reading the answer off of the projected image)
7	Teacher	If you don't want to write the actual word, what is the short form? A-M-T. Ok. AMT is a short form for amount. Not A-M-O – amo (said humorously while shaking her head). Then later on you say in plural, so amos (jokingly). (Students laughing.) And that is? Amos (saying it as a boy's name).
8	A student	Amos (repeating).
9	Teacher	Ok. So you should write down AMT – amount – and 20 cents – amount total. Then what do you mean by 50 cents? Is it clear enough? That is also an amount of money.

In Excerpt 1, we can see some common features of classroom talk: The teacher manages the class by asking students to raise and lower their hands (turns 1, 3, 5); the teacher comments on individual answers and compliments them on their correct responses, *very good* (turns 3, 5). The teacher also gives instructions (turn 9, *So you should write . . .*), makes comments about their learning (turn 1, *If you follow the method . . .*) and gives explanations (turn 5, *Ok, the next thing is we will have to make sure . . .*). In fact, one of the most common features of classroom talk is amply in evidence – the teacher does most of the talking. Students give short answers in response to teacher questions and students ask very few, if any, of their own questions. In addition, the teacher usually asks questions to which she knows the answer, so the questions are not *genuine* (in the sense that the teacher needs information which the student has, but the teacher does not know). These types of questions are often referred to as **display questions** since they ask students to display their knowledge rather than present new information or explore ideas. Teacher questions can also function to direct the classroom conversation along particular lines that the teacher wants to follow. In turn 5, for example, the teacher asks *Amount? Where is the amount?* while directing students to look at the projected information. Obviously the teacher already knows the answer and is using this question to check whether the students know the answer.

There are also some features of Excerpt 1 that are specific to mathematics classes, especially in terms of the academic or disciplinary content: They are talking about calculations for money, and they are talking about how to construct and read a table that shows the calculations for coins of different quantity (50 cent coins and 20 cent coins). This is why the teacher asks *Where is the amount?* in turn 5 – she is teaching them the calculations as well as how to present calculations using a table. The teacher also does something which might be rather unusual for a mathematics class – she incorporates information about the language which is needed. She refers to spelling and proper abbreviations in turn 7 and plays with the morphology (see Chapter 2) by imagining a plural form which changes the incorrect abbreviation (*amo*) into a boy's name *Amos* (turn 7). Throughout the teacher uses humour and encourages the students to laugh and enjoy the jokes – something that varies quite a lot from teacher to teacher. In this case, the use of humour helps to highlight some of the teaching points (use of correct mathematical abbreviations) and helps to keep the students engaged in what could otherwise be a mundane correction task.

Even in this brief example, it is clear that teachers use talk for a variety of purposes: engaging, explaining, correcting. Thus we can see that teacher talk is instructional as well as organizational; teachers use talk to purposefully work toward achieving educational goals. Talk is also socializing: It is a tool used to set up relationships and establish a communication system among language users. However, within the classroom teachers use this tool in ways that are different to our daily conversations. For one thing, in classroom talk, the topic is usually set by the teacher. The teacher orchestrates and steers the responses, determines who is going to contribute and provides feedback on student contributions (turn 5, *very good* but also turn 7, the correction of the form of abbreviation). Notice also that student contributions are bounded before and after by the teacher. Because of the quantity of talk by teachers and the way teachers use talk to control the lesson (and the students), classroom talk is considered to be **asymmetrical**.

The most common pattern for enacting these asymmetrical interactions is the **IRF** (or **IRE**) pattern – initiation, response and feedback/evaluation. In this chapter we will use IRF from this point on for the sake of consistency. The IRF sequence may be thought of as the traditional classroom interaction pattern. We can see it throughout Excerpt 1. It can be very useful for keeping the lesson moving, keeping the discussion on topic, controlling student interactions and doing quick checks of student knowledge. The downside is that it limits student opportunities to comment, explain, explore and ask questions. Within the IRF sequence, teachers tend to ask display questions which encourage short responses and factual information, rather than asking questions such as *Why do you think so?* and *How do you know that?* Questions such as *Tell me more about that.* or *Can you give me an example?* tend to be used infrequently. Heavy use of the IRF sequence limits how many students can talk within a lesson (since teachers typically call on students one by one), and thus can also limit whose ideas are heard and who gets feedback. However, the IRF sequence is not good or bad teaching on its own – it has both strengths and weaknesses. One problem with the IRF sequence is that it tends to be a teacher's default option – so classroom interaction is restricted to this one model – unless the teacher makes a deliberate change and uses some other interactional patterns.

Apart from IRF sequence, what are some other options? One option is to alter the evaluative aspect of the teacher's response. In her classic book *Classroom Discourse: The Language of Teaching and Learning*, Courtney Cazden (2001) shows examples from several mathematics lessons in which the teachers encourage students to give their own explanations and to express agreement/disagreement. In these cases, the teacher still manages the interaction but students have more opportunity to talk (quantity) and more opportunity to use language for different functions – although this can still result in short student responses. We see some of this in Excerpt 2, a pre-reading discussion of a passage about preserved foods, from a primary grade 5 lesson.

Excerpt 2 Preserved foods (English language lesson)

1	Teacher	. . . this morning I have umm prepared a lesson for you so umm let's look at the slides first and I would like you to think about what you are going to read OK? (The teacher shows a picture with jars of pickles, dried noodles and fish, a package of soup mix and a jar of instant coffee.)
2	Jacqueline	Food.
3	Teacher	Right. Hmm. Let's take a look at these. What are these?
4	Thomas	Food.
	Mala	Tupperware.
	Jaslyn	Mee goreng. ['Mee goreng' is a popular noodle dish in Singapore.]
5	Teacher	(Laughing) Which one?
6	Jaslyn	I eat mee goreng.
7	Teacher	Mee goreng? Yeah, so, umm. Why do you think? OK. I know you are excited over the food. Too bad you can't eat it now. OK. Umm. Chris, Chris, what do you think all these food here that you see have in common?
8	Chris	Preserving.
9	Teacher	Preserving? OK, now let's take a look at the jars over there, the jars over there. What are they?
10	Students	Pickle.
11	Teacher	Pickles. Have you tried them before?
12	Students	Yes/No
13	Teacher	How do they taste?
14	Chris	Very difficult to eat.
15	Teacher	Very difficult, why?
16	Chris	Sour.
17	Teacher	Ahah. It doesn't smell good. OK.
18	Sharlene	Very very salty.
19	Teacher	You got to hold your breath when you bite, is it?
20	Faizal	And then my father ah (undecipherable from recording).
21	Teacher	OK. Aisha, you say it's nice? (Laughs) OK, good. So we . . . Different people have got different tastes.

In Excerpt 2, we can see some differences to Excerpt 1. To encourage the students to share their experiences and ideas in preparation for reading, the teacher shows a few images on the projector with pictures of preserved foods. Notice that in turn 2, a student quickly picks up the topic and starts to comment even before the teacher asks any questions. In turn 3, we again see a display question *What are these?*, referring to the items in the picture. However, since there are several items, there are several possible answers, as in turn 4. The teacher laughs, perhaps at all the excited responses, and asks *Which one?* looking at the student who said *mee goreng*. Since mee goreng is a popular noodle dish in Singapore, it is most likely that the teacher understands what the student says; however, the picture shows dried, instant noodles in a package so the teacher might be asking the student to expand on the answer a bit. The student does expand, slightly, in turn 6 by making the sentence *I eat mee goreng*. The teacher response (turn 7) does not offer evaluation or feedback but seems to be simply an acknowledgement *Mee goreng? Yeah, so umm.*

Subsequently we see a few more display questions in which the teacher successfully moves the discussion along to the idea of preserving. Then the teacher shifts to asking the students about their personal experiences (turn 11 onwards). Although the student replies are very short indeed (turns 12, 14, 16, 18), we also see that they are *authentic* in the sense that they are the students' own ideas and experiences which they contribute to the discussion. The teacher's reaction is to continue to probe for more information rather than evaluate the answers given. In these ways, the classroom interaction in Excerpt 2 is somewhat different to Excerpt 1.

Other options for teacher talk

How might the teacher encourage even more extended replies? When we look more closely at the types of teacher questions in Excerpt 2, we see that she asks questions which are quite factually based: *What are these? What do they have in common? Have you tried them before? How do they taste?* Although these questions give students the opportunity to offer their own experiences and ideas, they don't encourage the children to explain their opinions or examine their own thinking. For the most part, these are what Mehan (1979) calls **choice questions** – students can reply from among a set of possible choices (yes/no, either/or, or from a limited list of options).

Other possible question types suggested by Mehan are process and metaprocess questions. **Process questions** ask students to give opinions, interpretations and explanations. For example, at turn 15 the teacher asks

Very difficult, why? encouraging the student to provide some explanation. Questions with *how* and *why*, which probe for more information from students, can provide an opportunity for teachers to better understand student knowledge, and for students to use more expanded language – but as we see in turn 16, there is no guarantee that students will take up the opportunity. **Metaprocess questions** address students' knowledge processes – *How do you know that?* is a possible metaprocess question. Metaprocess questions can help us understand not only what students know or don't know, but also what they know about their own learning. Unfortunately, these questions tend to be used very infrequently in classrooms.

So far we have been focusing on different question types, but teachers have other options as well. Some research on mathematics lessons has shown that by setting problems for students and then asking them to explain the method they used to solve the problems, teachers can encourage extended explanations and the expression of mathematical thinking. We can envision this if we go back to Excerpt 1 and imagine that instead of the *teacher* showing the student's work (turn 5), highlighting specific points and commenting, she could ask the *student* to share and explain his own work.

The teacher can also set up **sharing time** (Cazden, 2001), a context in which, albeit briefly, students can take on the role of expert and engage in more extended talk. You can imagine this as a primary school personal sharing (e.g. *Tell us about what you did this weekend*) or a secondary grade science lesson (e.g. *Tell us how you did the experiment and what you found out*). While students are responsible for the sharing, teachers can offer support if students stumble. Teachers can also provide feedback after sharing is completed, similar to an IRF.

Teachers can also change the dynamic of the classroom interaction by attempting to engage in more **dialogic teaching**. Dialogic teaching encourages ongoing talk between teacher and students rather than continuous teacher talk in class. It is intended to be an approach to using classroom talk for learning rather than a specific method. In particular, dialogic teaching can make use of all of the types of talk introduced above, but it also encourages discussion with an open exchange of ideas – an exchange which explores student thinking, issues and problems (Alexander, 2008). Teachers are expected to use talk to help students build on each other's ideas (not just respond to the teacher's idea), to extend student contributions (not just evaluate) and to encourage thinking through consideration of a variety of possibilities (not just accepting 'the right answer'). Excerpts 3a and 3b demonstrates some of the key principles of dialogic talk. Both of these excerpts are from the same lesson – a primary grade 4 discussion about a children's book on ants.

In Excerpt 3a the teacher initially asked, *So most of you can see that it is a picture of two ants. What do you know about ants? Can anyone tell me? What do you know about ants?* Subsequently there is discussion of facts about ants and features of ants bodies. We read from a midpoint when the teacher calls on a student saying, *Ok Rasyid.*

Excerpt 3a Ants (English language lesson)

1	Rasyid	Ants can climb up.
2	Teacher	Ants can climb up? Climb up where?
3	Emily	The wall.
4	Teacher	Climb up the wall? Ok. Cannot? Can or cannot? (Some students are saying 'yes', 'no', 'can', 'cannot'.) Why do you say so? Ok why do you say that they cannot climb?
5	Sharmila	Can.
6	Teacher	Ah? Now you say 'can'? Don't worry I already told you there's no right, there's no wrong, ok? So what do you think now? Can they climb?
7	Alfred	Can.
8	Teacher	Ants can climb up. Ok. Ok yes?
9	Unidentified student	(inaudible)
10	Teacher	Some ants have wings. Interesting idea. Do you know which ants have wings? (Student shakes his head.) Don't know? Ok, you?
11	Mei	Some ants lay eggs.
12	Teacher	Some ants lay eggs! Good. Yes?
13	Unidentified student	(inaudible)
14	Teacher	Ants have mouth. They have mouth, this one? (points to an image from the book). Ok. What else?

From these exchanges, and throughout the transcript, we can see that the classroom conversation is *collective* (with everyone working toward the same task), *reciprocal* (with students sharing ideas) and *supportive* (with an emphasis on helping each other rather than correcting 'wrong' answers). This is especially evident in turn 6 when the teacher explicitly states the supportive principle, and in turn 10 when the teacher does not correct or explain but accepts that the student might not know the answer and carries on with the discussion.

The reciprocal principle also requires that students are allowed to agree, disagree and share their different views. We see this in the continuation of the lesson as in Excerpt 3b from turn 15 onwards where there is some disagreement about eyes/feelers. In turn 19 the teacher points out that the students should listen to each other and throughout the teacher shows that it is ok to disagree.

Excerpt 3b Ants continued

15	Teacher	Ants can grow? No, no, no? Ants have eyes. They have eyes, they have mouth.
16	Mark	No! They have feelers.
17	Teacher	Marcus disagree with you. He said ants don't have eyes. They have feelers. What do you think?
18	Steven	I know, I know.
19	Teacher	Now Marcus said that he disagrees with . . . your idea. You said they have eyes right? Marcus said they have feelers. Put all your hands down. Listen to this. We are discussing this point now.
20	Mark	Teacher, it's not Marcus. It's Mark.
21	Teacher	Mark. Oh ok. Mark said he disagrees with your friend over there. He said ants have eyes. Mark said no they have feelers. What do you all say? Eyes or no eyes?
22	Evelyn	Got eyes what.[a]
23	Teacher	Who says ants have eyes? Put up your hands? Ok. Who says ants have no eyes? Who says I don't know whether ants have eyes or not?
24	Students in chorus	Me.
25	Teacher	Very good. Ah . . . Some of you say 'don't have eyes'. Some of you say 'have eyes'. Some of you say 'don't know'. So who doesn't know?
26	Sophia	Teacher! I (inaudible).
27	Geok Leng	Ants have eyes but cannot see. They use their feelers.
28	Teacher	Ants have eyes but they cannot see. They use their feelers to feel wherever they are. Ok, interesting idea! You see some of you say 'yes'. Some of you say 'no'. Some of you say 'don't know'. So today from this lesson, we are going to find out a bit more about ants. The thing is a lot of you already know a lot of things about ants, right? Yeah? So what do you think we will find out today, yeah? So let's see. So today we are going to read this book.

[a] This is a grammatical form used in informal Singapore English to disagree. It is not a question, but a statement. There is some discussion of language varieties in Chapter 4, though not specific to Singapore English.

In the end, the teacher does not give the answer but acknowledges that there are different ideas and more information is needed (turn 28). The teacher also uses this turn to move to the next activity – reading a book about ants (turn 28). This shows another principle of dialogic teaching – it is *purposeful*. Although the discussion is open-ended, it moves toward a common purpose. To some extent the conversation is also *cumulative* – it encourages the students to build on each other's ideas – however, we note that the excerpt is not particularly strong in this area as the teacher does a lot of the work of chaining the comments together, rather than the students doing it them-selves. If students were to chain comments together effectively, we might see more extended student turns as well. As in Excerpts 3a and 3b, although student turns are frequent and thoughtful, with students contributing their own ideas, we see quite short turns with fairly simple sentence structure. This is most likely influenced by the task: State what you know about ants. In this case, students are not required to present reasons, work through complex arguments or talk about hypothetical situations, so it is not surprising that the language used is mostly simple statements. The brevity of the responses might also be due to the fact that the students are consistently talking to the teacher who is the final authority on everything said.

Truly dialogic teaching would address all five principles: collective, reciprocal, supportive, cumulative and purposeful. This is quite different from the traditional IRF sequence. However, it is important to stress again that no one is saying all classroom conversations should be dialogic or sharing or any other set pattern. The concern is that teachers adjust the classroom talk to suit the educational goals, at the same time recognizing the different ways in which language is used in these classroom conversations.

Yet another way to change classroom conversations is to move the teacher out of the conversation and set up peer work (pair, trio or group). So let's look at peer conversations in educational settings.

How do students use talk in classrooms?

In this section we look at how students use talk in the classroom, focussing on peer interaction and types of student talk. We discuss the benefits of peer talk and how teachers can identify types of talk within such interactions.

Student talk in groups

Working in small groups provides students with the opportunity to 'make connections, re-arrange, reconceptualize and internalize the new experiences, ideas and ways of knowing' (Barnes, 1992, p. 6). Since language is the most common medium for classroom learning, students need to be given sufficient time to talk through new knowledge presented to them in classes and to make it their own. Barnes has identified two functions of speech in the classroom – presentational and exploratory. **Presentational talk** is used to demonstrate an acceptable performance rather than explore a topic. Presentational talk is not used to *develop* an understanding, but to *demonstrate* understanding, for example, to provide a 'right' answer. We saw many examples in the excerpts above.

However, when students cooperate on a task, they will have more opportunities to engage in **exploratory talk**. This type of talk might be in a tentative manner (e.g. *I think we should . . . What if we . . .? Do you think . . .?*) as the students consider and rearrange their ideas. It can be hesitant and contain incomplete utterances as students try to express their developing understandings. While the student talk might seem to be less fluent or less accurate, it is important for students to have the opportunity to work through new concepts – this can often be accomplished in peer conversations. While working in peer groups, there can be an exchange of ideas, information and opinions which does not happen as frequently in traditional, teacher-fronted instruction. Quality cooperative work must provide opportunities for students to talk and work together towards meaning making by posing questions, making observations, contributing opinions, etc.

Types of student talk

Student talk is seen as a 'valuable tool for the joint construction of knowledge' (Mercer et al., 2010, p. 370). However, just as teacher talk can be structured differently to provide different opportunities for student to engage in the classroom conversation, so can student peer talk vary in quantity and quality. Before we can determine if peer talk is valuable or beneficial, we should at least have an idea of how to identify different possible types of student talk in the classroom. Neil Mercer has done extensive research on talk in classrooms. He has proposed a framework for three types of talk in which children can engage in classes: exploratory, cumulative or disputational. He proposes that **exploratory talk** is most likely to facilitate learning. When students cooperate and think together using exploratory talk, they help each other 'share knowledge, evaluate evidence and consider options in a reasonable and equitable way' (Mercer, 2002, p. 150). This is because in exploratory talk, students' knowledge and reasoning, ideas and understandings are publicly expressed. Exploratory talk includes offering opinions, giving reasons to support the opinions shared, seeking each other's views and checking agreement. As you can see, this aligns closely with the ideas of dialogical talk discussed above. In fact, this kind of talk is the foundation for dialogic teaching which allow students to use language to make sense of and engage in complex interactions.

What about the two other types of talk in Mercer's framework? **Disputational talk** is talk in which 'disagreements and individualized decision making' (1996, p. 369) are present. This typically consists of short exchanges of assertions and challenges or counter assertions. **Cumulative talk** is characterized as talk that 'builds positively but uncritically' (1996, p. 369) on what others have said. This typically includes repetitions and confirmations (e.g. *uh huh*, *I get you*), and might include elaborations (in which students elaborate on ideas, sometimes using more complex sentences to put ideas together). While disputational talk might allow students to express alternative opinions, it provides few opportunities for students to build on each other's ideas or language. Cumulative talk does allow some use of language to build on each other's ideas but might lack depth of thinking due to its uncritical nature.

It is important to note that having the opportunity to engage in more exploratory talk doesn't necessarily mean that students do so. For example, putting students in groups with peers will not automatically lead to productive talk (in the sense of talk which explains, explores or critiques ideas or in the sense of language which requires rich vocabulary or complex grammar). In Excerpt 4, the students have been asked to work at a common table to share materials and create masks. Later, they will write about the steps used to create their masks, and then present the masks and the procedural text to their classmates.

Excerpt 4 Making Masks (English language lesson)

1	Cheryl	Glue the . . . this one first. Glue it.
2	Li Fan	Yeah.
3	Aria	How do I know what to do?
4	Li Fan	So heavy, isn't it?
5	Cheryl	Ok, next step. What can I do?
6	Li Fan	How do I know what to do?
7	Rashida	Can I have your (inaudible)?
8	Cheryl	Today is your birthday?
9	Rashida	No. Eh, can you (inaudible)?
10	Aria	Yeah.
11	Li Fan	This is . . . cute, right?
12	Cheryl	On Saturday. On Sunday is Mala's birthday.
13	Rashida	I know.
14	Cheryl	And on Tuesday is my birthday.
15	Rashida	I know.

In Excerpt 4, we see that students do not talk much, and do not necessarily talk about the work they are doing. Their speech tends to be simple in terms of vocabulary and grammatical structures. From this excerpt we can see that while the students do cooperate in preparing their notice and they do use different types of talk, the task itself does not require much in the way of explanation, opinions or substantial ideas. This suggests that teachers should think carefully about the types of tasks they ask their students to do and the types of language that might be used to accomplish those tasks. Teachers must also model and encourage different types of talk in their own interactions with students (see, also, Chapter 6).

RELEVANCE TO EDUCATIONAL SETTINGS

In this chapter we discussed how language is used in classrooms – including in subjects other than language classes – and presented features of teacher and student talk. Let's recap why this matters:

When we ask students to explain how something works in a science class, for example, we are not only asking for scientific knowledge; we are also asking for particular kinds of language structures and vocabulary that suit our idea of what a scientific explanation should be. (See Chapter 6 on disciplinary literacy.) Sometimes the difficulty for students is not the scientific content, but the language to express their ideas. As teachers in any academic subject, we might need to support students' language needs as well as their academic content knowledge. This can be done by actively teaching vocabulary, modelling the appropriate use of language in your subject area and sometimes by explicitly teaching students to use language in particular ways for specific academic subjects.

As a teacher, you should also consider if, when and how you use different types of classroom interactions: IRF, sharing, dialogic teaching and peer work. Do you use IRF disproportionally? If so, for what purposes? Is this something you want to maintain or try to change in order to achieve specific educational objectives? Also consider the types of activities and tasks you set for your students – whether in whole-class format or for peer work. It is easy to tell students to work together, it is not so easy to set tasks which require cooperation (i.e. in which students must cooperate in order to complete the task), encourage different types of talk (disputational, cumulative, exploratory) and provide opportunities for sharing substantial ideas, opinions and explanations. A discussion of tasks would require a whole book, but even without a book to offer suggestions, you can examine activities you set as peer work and ask yourself these questions:

If I were a student, how would I do this?

What might be the problems?

What might I say to my partner?

Does this task require me to:

describe?

explain?

offer opinions?

give reasons?

When you are teaching, you can take this a step further by listening to how your students use language during peer work – not just listening to see if they are on task, but listening in detail to how they use language to do the task. This will give you ideas about how to adjust the task in subsequent lessons. This type of thoughtful examination of student work in progress will help you to better understand learner needs and to continue your professional development.

DISCUSSION AND REFLECTION QUESTIONS

1   Reread Excerpt 1 and consider other ways the teacher might work with the student's example. Consider how the lesson might develop if the student presented his own work, for example. What might be the advantages? The possible problems? What type of language would the student need to use? How could the teacher help to support the student in presenting his ideas?

2   Reflect on the classes you have been engaged in for the past week (as a student or as a teacher). Would you say that the classes have been mostly teacher-fronted, peer work or something else? Why do you think the lessons were conducted in this way? How might your learning have been impacted by the types of interaction in the lessons?

3   Consider the idea of exploratory talk. In your opinion what are some of the pros and cons of exploratory talk in a language lesson? In a science lesson? How might use of tasks which encourage exploratory

talk influence English language learners – would these types of tasks make it easier or more difficult for students to engage in classroom conversations? What might be the advantages/disadvantages for students in terms of language learning?

RECOMMENDED READING AND VIEWING

Cazden's book is a classic discussion of classroom interaction. It has lots of examples, excellent explanations and provides food for thought for teachers.

    Cazden, C. (2001), *Classroom Discourse: The Language of Teaching and Learning* (2nd edn). Portsmouth, NH: Heinemann.

Robin Alexander is a major proponent of dialogic teaching. He has quite a few books and articles on the topic. This online summary is a good overview:

    Alexander, R. (n.d.), *Dialogic Teaching Essentials*. Available at: www.nie.edu.sg/files/oer/FINAL%20Dialogic%20Teaching%20Essentials.pdf

    You can find more, including video and examples, at this website: www.teachfind.com/national-strategies/dialogic-talk

For those who want to know more about how language and academic content are integrated for English-language learners, the Center for Applied Linguistics has prepared a digest which summarizes the key ideas. You might find some of their other digests useful as well.

    Sherris, A. (2008), *Integrated content and language instruction*. *CAL Digest*. Washington, DC: Center for Applied Linguistics. Available at: www.cal.org/resources/digest/integratedcontent.html

You can find out more about cooperative learning at the Daily Teaching Tools website. There is an explanation of cooperative learning along with suggested activities/tasks that you can use in your teaching. Go to:

    www.dailyteachingtools.com/cooperative-learning.html

8

How Do People Use Different Languages Differently?

Manka M. Varghese and Rukmini Becerra Lubies

INTRODUCTION

In this chapter, we address the concept of bilingualism. Bilingualism in its simplest definition refers to the ability to use at least two languages, varieties or codes. The ability to use multiple languages can refer to children and adults who are already using both languages or are learning additional languages. Moreover, these languages can be learned and adopted by users of the **majority language** or users of a **minority language**. The reason we are choosing the word *use* rather than *speak* is that bilinguals can use one or more of the different skills of speaking, listening, reading and writing, as well as vary in their proficiency in these skills.

Along with understanding that bilinguals' proficiency in and their usage of two languages is complex, it is also important to view bilinguals as involved in a holistic process of bilingualism, not solely negotiating two monolingual codes, as we will discuss. For many bilinguals or emergent bilinguals, they have not necessarily had the same types of exposure in the two languages, or they might prefer using these two languages for different reasons and with different interlocutors and in different settings. For bilinguals, these two languages are viewed as interacting cognitively and often socially rather than acting in isolation to each other; in other words, one language will influence the other in various ways.

We view bilingualism as an asset and, in the same vein as García (2009), advocate bilingualism as a way of promoting equity as well as strength in communities of majority and minority speakers. In this chapter, we underscore the social definition of bilingualism and the fact that it cannot be separated from its speakers and the contexts in which it is used. We start by reviewing the main definitions of a bilingual individual and the routes people follow to become bilingual. Then, we discuss the language practices of bilinguals, which is an important window into examining how bilingualism is socially enacted. Next, we consider how bilingual students' needs are addressed in schools, as well as the roles of families and the wider society in bilingualism. In all these sections, we show how the consideration of multiple as well as societal factors changes *traditional* conceptions of bilingualism. The importance of these social factors lies in the fact that there is no language without community. People interact with their languages while, at the same time, they evaluate the languages and the speakers of the languages. Therefore, examining language communities and the contexts in which bilingualism exists is crucial in understanding this phenomenon.

WHO IS A BILINGUAL?

It is now well known that bilingualism affects people's linguistic, academic and cognitive skills in positive ways. It is viewed as having a number of **cognitive benefits**, for example, it enhances cognitive functioning (a process of becoming aware of and understanding ideas), memory and brain plasticity (the way experiences reorganize mental pathways). Moreover, bilingualism augments cognitive flexibility due to the two different ways bilinguals experience, perceive and think about an idea or concept. Bialystok (2011) argues that the major empirical finding of the positive effects of bilingualism on cognition is the evidence of enhanced **executive control** in bilinguals and that this has been validated in numerous studies. This means that bilinguals use the executive control aspect of cognitive functioning to select and use the language they need as they are evaluating the environment and interlocutors around them. Bialystok and others (Craik, Bialystok and Freedman, 2010) hypothesize that this may be one of the reasons that bilingualism may have a protective function for diseases such as Alzheimer's.

Historically, as we mentioned earlier, bilinguals were viewed as two monolinguals in one person. A newer view conceives of bilinguals as holistic and complete individuals. Let's review the main ideas for these two perspectives. In this section, we also summarize notions related to the identification of who is a bilingual, and who is not, although these definitions have been contested.

From a traditional perspective, a bilingual person has the same control of two languages as a monolingual speaker does of one language in all contexts and with all individuals (Bloomfield, 1933). For instance, a Spanish-English bilingual speaks Spanish as a Spanish monolingual and speaks English as an English monolingual. The term that describes this situation is **balanced bilingual**. Nevertheless, these people do not truly exist. The idea of balanced bilingual might be useful for research purposes, but it becomes problematic when used to categorize real people and their language skills. In real situations, people use two languages in different contexts with different participants and for different purposes. For instance, a common scenario is someone who speaks one language at home and another one at work. In this instance, the bilingual does not have the same vocabulary in each language, does not use the same linguistic strategies and does not have the same language skills. Another common scenario is someone who speaks both languages at the same time – usually when talking to someone else who knows both languages. Therefore, establishing that one person has identical competence in two languages is a difficult task. Critics of the term 'balanced bilingual' argue, for example, that a physician from Thailand may have a complete knowledge of the English vocabulary used in medicine, but only basic vocabulary to talk about sports in English.

If a balanced bilingual is someone who has equal control of two languages, traditionalists define someone who does not have full competence in either of the two languages as **semilingual**. The semilingual notion has been criticized as well. First, as above, this notion does not consider that bilinguals use their languages for different purposes. Young children might have full linguistic competence in their second language in the school context, but less linguistic competence in their second language in a religious context. Second, the term 'semilingual' defines individuals from a deficit perspective; the term 'semi' implies that these speakers are not 'complete'. In addition, it seems to make the individual responsible for not being 'fully' bilingual and implies that the person lacks the necessary cognitive skills. This ignores any responsibility of schools or wider society to provide resources to become bilingual. This notion also conceives of bilingualism solely as an internal process which occurs inside the individual's brain; it does not consider the social, economic and political factors that affect bilingualism. To sum up, both the terms 'balanced' and 'semilingual' are based on a false comparison between bilinguals and monolinguals. This is especially worth noting in that the majority of the world population is bilingual and to consider monolinguals as the group that bilinguals should 'imitate' is making the assumption that they are the norm, which is not the case.

In contrast, Grosjean (1985) has proposed a holistic view of bilinguals. In his view, a bilingual person is an integrated whole (one person) with multicompetencies, not two monolinguals. Bilinguals are unique; they have their own characteristics, skills and mental processes. With this in mind, a broader definition of bilingualism has been proposed. This includes

> not only the 'perfect' bilingual (who probably does not exist) or the 'balanced' bilingual (who is probable rare), but also various 'imperfect' and 'unstable' forms of bilingualism, in which one language takes over from the other(s) on at least some occasions and for some instances of language use. (in Dewaele, 2007, p. 104)

Incipient neurological evidence supports the view that bilinguals are unique in how they process language. PET and MRI scans have identified cognitive processing differences of bilinguals as well as differences in how information may be organized and retrieved for bilinguals versus monolinguals. Some important observations have been that

- there seems to be more right-hemisphere brain activity when bilinguals process language (versus monolinguals);
- bilingual aphasics lose and recover each language differently. (Aphasia is a loss or impairment of language competency due to brain damage.)

As we can see, defining who is and who is not a bilingual is not straight-forward. Definitions are important for understanding complicated pheno-menon, but simple categorizations are inappropriate for describing the multiple levels and distinctions of bilingualism. Another level of complexity in bilingualism is examining the route of how people learn languages. We discuss this in the next section.

LEARNING TWO LANGUAGES

Some individuals acquire two or more languages in their earliest childhood, while others become bilinguals later through schooling and study. The first situation is referred to as **simultaneous bilingualism** and the second as **sequential bilingualism**. However, some scholars have noted that these concepts have not worked as well in the twenty-first century, since children are often involved in multilingual situations at school. A more useful distinction might be 'childhood bilinguals', those who become bilingual in childhood, and emerging bilingualism, those who develop bilingualism later.

Although the processing and ultimate proficiency in both languages may not be equivalent, simultaneous bilinguals do achieve high levels of proficiency in both languages. For example, the pronunciation of a simultaneous bilingual can be the same as that of a monolingual in each language. In addition, other studies have shown that simultaneous bilinguals develop higher levels of metalinguistic awareness – the ability to reflect on the nature and use of language – earlier than monolinguals. For instance, Bialystok (1987) found that at an early age bilingual children can count words in a sentence, a task that a monolingual manages at a later age. Also, bilinguals have been found to be more analytical about the structure of both languages in which they are competent.

Much of the research on childhood bilingualism has pointed to the ability of infants to discriminate the differences between languages, and remember the information in these languages. In Genesee's review (2003), he states that the rate of the emergence of certain linguistic aspects is comparable for bilinguals and monolinguals. What may be different is that bilinguals are able to produce mixed utterances in addition to monolingual ones at an early age. It is worth noting, as above, that in many parts of the world, childhood bilingualism is the norm.

In terms of sequential bilingualism and emergent bilingualism, one of the central foci has been the concern that there may be a **critical period** for language learning (see Chapter 5), and this is also a concern for those who start learning a second language later in life. One school of thought is that second language learning becomes difficult after the age of 7, or, at least, it is not possible to achieve the same proficiency as someone who started learning before the age of 5. In contrast, another proposal is that older children can learn a second language better and faster as they can make use of metalinguistic awareness from their first language and their superior cognitive processing system. For instance, 15-year-old students knows what a noun, verb or adjective is. They also know that words have meanings. Therefore, if a teacher in a Spanish second language class says that the common grammar structure is noun + adjective, these students have a better chance to understand the language structure as compared to a 6-year-old child who is just starting to learn grammar about a language.

What seems clear is that considering age as the only critical factor in the development of sequential language learning presents a simplistic view of becoming bilingual. Other factors have been identified as crucial in this process. These include length and quality of exposure to the second language, social context and support to learn the second language (see Chapter 5). Genesee (2004) states that especially when discussing bilingualism in schools, the proficiency in both languages has more to do with student and pedagogical factors than anything else. Some of these student factors might include their literacy levels, educational background, their socio-economic status, while the pedagogical factors may include the teaching methods used as well as the amount of exposure to the second language in schools.

CODESWITCHING AND TRANSLANGUAGING

When conceptualizing the complexity of how bilingualism actually unfolds in social situations, the concepts of **codeswitching** and **translanguaging** are critical to consider. 'Codeswitching' refers to the switching of two languages in a specific conversation. While there is not a universal agreement about why people codeswitch, many agree that switching is triggered by the participants, the context, the topic and purpose of the conversation. For example, bilinguals switch to (a) emphasize a point in a conversation, (b) express a concept that does not have an equivalent in the other language, (c) clarify or expand on a sentence, (d) express their identity, (e) change attitudes or relationship, (f) include and exclude people from a conversation or (g) discuss specific topics (Baker, 2011). Most importantly, codeswitching, far from being a mechanism to deal with language deficit, actually occurs more often in conversations between fluent bilinguals. This suggests that codeswitching is a resource, a special competence of bilinguals, and not a type of language interference, or confusion, of individuals (García, 2009). This is a case of bilinguals using their full linguistic resources to enable a conversation and fulfil certain goals in the conversation.

One of the most interesting findings about codeswitching is that it is not random speech but is governed by grammatical regularities. What is more, speakers who codeswitch can recognize when some switches are grammatical or ungrammatical. For instance, bilingual speakers have been asked to evaluate various exchanges where codeswitching may occur and they have been able to identify which are grammatical and authentic and which are not. Second, the social status of the languages influences code-switching. When the languages involved in a conversation with bilinguals have asymmetrical status, codeswitching is asymmetrical too. It has been observed that among Swedish Americans and Mexican Americans in the USA, the switch occurs only from the less prestigious language to the **dominant language**, the dominant language being English in this case. For instance, a Swedish American may say *jag ska JOINA er sen*, instead of *Jag* *ska ansluta mig till er sen*, which translates, *I will join you later*. Third, the study of codeswitching has also provided relevant information about how the brain of bilinguals manage two languages. In the past, it was assumed that only one 'channel' could be involved in language production in bilinguals' brains. However, recent studies have demonstrated that when a bilingual hears or reads a word in one language, the corresponding expression in the other language is at least partially activated. In other words, even when a bilingual appears to be operating solely in one language, the brain storage for the other language is still passively involved.

Codeswitching is included in translanguaging, but translanguaging includes all ways of using multiple languages from the perspectives of bilinguals. **Translanguaging** is a broad umbrella term that describes 'multilingual discursive practices in which bilinguals engage in order to make sense of their bilingual worlds' (García, 2009, p. 45). For example, translanguaging occurs in multilingual families and may be the main language practice of such families. It also occurs in many schools where minority children may read in English, for example, but then play using their other common language.

BILINGUALISM IN SCHOOLS

In the previous sections, we have reviewed three important themes related to bilingualism: who is a bilingual, the routes to being bilingual and bilingualism as a social practice through codeswitching and translanguaging. As implied above, people can become bilingual mainly due to family language use or due to schooling in two languages. Specifically, in this section we examine the role of schools in bilingualism.

Schools can promote or hinder bilingualism. One way in which schools can actually hinder bilingualism is through attempting to cut off the children's home language by arguing that in order to develop fluent proficiency in a second language, they need to give up their family language. In these schools, educators advise the parents to speak the school language at home. For instance, a Chinese family in France might be encouraged to speak French at home. However, Lambert (1987) found that the prohibition of speaking the home language does not improve the children's proficiency in the language spoken at school. On the contrary, the author found that the loss of the home language can have important negative consequences on the children's self-esteem, identity and also on their relationship with the members of the family. These situations negatively impact the academic learning of children. Because this reduces the child's bilingual learning opportunities, this is known as **subtractive bilingualism**. On the other hand, schools can promote bilingualism and individual achievement through **additive bilingualism**. In these cases, the home language is maintained at home while the school language is learned at school. Additive bilingualism has positive consequences for the children's self-esteem, identity and interaction with family members.

Another important aspect of the positive influence of one language on the other in school settings is that of transference in bilingualism, which can be seen as part of **skill transfer theory**. This theory proposes that the prior knowledge of learners influences positively the acquisition of new knowledge. Specifically, language and literacy skills can be transferred from first language to the second language in bilingual learners. This is related to Cummins (1978) **linguistic interdependence hypothesis**, which states that instruction in and promotion of a child's first language can lead to transfer to the second language. This principle has direct implications for schools and classrooms, since it suggests that learning to read in the first language is beneficial for the acquisition of reading skills in another language. His interdependence hypothesis led Cummins to propose that there is a **Common Underlying Proficiency (CUP)**. In this, he argues that the languages for bilinguals are not stored separately in the brain but have a common underlying linguistic proficiency. Moreover, although the specifics of the languages may be different from each other, they work together for the bilingual's overall linguistic proficiency. Thus, even when the linguistic structure of both languages may be dissimilar, the conceptual, literacy and world knowledge that a student has in one language can be transferred from one language to the other.

Two influential ideas that Cummins (1979) developed in relation to bilingualism in schools are **basic interpersonal communication skills (BICS)** and **cognitive academic language proficiency (CALP)**. These notions are widely used in bilingual education to describe the levels of proficiency of minority language learners. In his work, Cummins proposed that BICS refers to the ability of language minority children to speak fluently in informal contexts. On the other hand, CALP refers to the academic language developed within schooling and literacy contexts – often considered a high-order language skill. Furthermore, CALP is defined as the ability to use spoken and written language without relying on non-linguistic cues to convey complex meanings.

Although, these concepts are extensively used in the literature about bilingual education, some researchers have argued that BICS and CALP are problematic. In particular, it has been pointed out that the characteristics of CALP are not higher-order language skills as Cummins proposed, but rather CALP reflects the properties of language in one specific context: the school. In addition, the supposition that literacy is intrinsically a superior ability has been criticized. Recent views suggest that literacy should be viewed as a technology used to represent language graphically. Therefore, it has been proposed that CALP is not more developed or complex than BICS, but simply different. Rolstad and MacSwan (2008) propose instead the term **second language instructional competence**, which does not assign any cognitive superiority or higher status to language in schools. Second language instructional competence refers to the stages of second language development in which learners are able to understand instruction and perform grade-level school activities using the second language in a particular educational setting at a particular moment in time. According to these researchers, when students know enough of the second language to participate at that moment, in that setting and in that subject, they can be said to have second language instructional competence in that subject area. Therefore the competence in one language can lead to second language instructional competence in another language.

SOCIETAL BILINGUALISM

In this section, we review **societal bilingualism** and how societal factors affect bilingualism. In some societies, two languages can be used for different purposes, and in different contexts. It is common to find communities in which the 'High' variety of the language is used in public contexts such as school and work and the 'Low' variety is used in private contexts such as home and church. Ferguson (1959) defined this separation of High and Low varieties as **diglossia**. This is the case of Spanish and Guaraní in Paraguay, for example, where Spanish is used in public contexts and Guaraní (an indigenous language) is spoken in private contexts.

Noticing the strong connection between bilingual people and the societies in which they live, Fishman (1980) proposed integrating the notions of bilingualism and diglossia to describe ways in which these can interact within communities. In the first scenario, both bilingualism and diglossia exist at the same time in the same community. In this situation, the majority language is used for one set of purposes, and the minority language for another set of purposes, such as in Egypt where Classical Arabic is used for education and Colloquial Arabic for the home or the example of Paraguay provided above. A second situation describes communities in which diglossia exists without bilingualism. In this case, one group of inhabitants speaks one language and the other group speaks a different language. For example, in India many of the elite groups speak English as well as their home languages, whereas the rest of the population speak only the home languages without access to the High variety. A third case is bilingualism without diglossia. In this case, many use both languages in any context but there is no societal arrangement for the maintenance of the two languages, such as the USA and its many bilingual speakers. A fourth case is where there is neither bilingualism nor diglossia, which is rare, but can refer sometimes to communities which were bilingual but were forced to become monolinguals. One example is the case of Cuba, where the indigenous language was eliminated.

While diglossia is not present in all bilingual communities, bilingualism is widely spread in the world. In fact, bilingualism is a reality for millions of people. It has been estimated that at least roughly half of the global population is bilingual (Grosjean, 1982). This bilingualism occurs in many different ways. In Canada, bilinguals speak English or French, and either of these is the majority or minority language depending on the region. In Israel, individuals speak Arabic or English and Hebrew. In Ireland, many speak Irish and English. In South American countries, such as Peru and Ecuador, indigenous groups generally use their indigenous language along with Spanish.

As you may already be aware, historical as well as political and societal characteristics also influence how bilingualism has evolved in society. Changes that have occurred in numerous countries (e.g. the USA, Switzerland, Singapore, Africa) with regard to bilingual education show that societal characteristics and political decisions can promote or inhibit bilingualism. When societies are supportive of bilingualism, bilingualism becomes a key component in these countries. In other words, individuals are more likely to become bilingual when they live in countries with policies that support bilingualism (see Chapter 9).

When societies are not as supportive of bilingualism, families play an even more crucial role. In this situation, we encounter cases of either immigrant parents wanting their children to learn their home language as well as learn the dominant language, not emphasizing their home languages, or in some instances actively try to remove the home language from children's learning environments. There may be cultural and/or economic reasons for parents to want to maintain both languages for their children while for those who either do not actively pursue the maintenance of both languages or reject the use of the home language for their children; they might be incorrectly assuming that the knowledge of the home language will interfere with the learning of the dominant language.

The case of parents wanting to make their children bilingual when they themselves are not usually refers to situations in which parents from a high socio-economic status (SES) decide to enrol their children in bilingual programs. In doing this, these children receive the professional and economic advantages of bilingualism, such as, studying abroad or working in an international company. This type of bilingualism is called **elitist bilingualism** (Lanza, 2007). An example would be a family who live in Korea, an officially monolingual country, teaching English to their children in order to give them the opportunity to study in England or the USA. However, Lanza (2007) indicates that while this categorization is real, the term 'elitist' is inaccurate as it does not consider the challenges that parents have to face to educate their children as bilinguals. In fact, not only high SES families want their children to become bilingual, but also parents in middle- and working-class families. These families might use different and more affordable resources to teach their children a second language. One of these resources is television materials using cartoons and movies which are designed to teach two languages. The question is whether these resources are effective. In noticing that these media resources are widely used by parents, Patricia Kuhl and her colleagues ran a series of experiments to study the effectiveness of these materials (2004). She exposed two groups of children to Mandarin as a second language. One of the groups interacted in person with a Mandarin speaker and the second group watched a Mandarin speaker on television. After some sessions, Kuhl found that only the group of children who interacted with the Mandarin speaker in person learned Mandarin (see Chapter 5).

Although families are part of society, some scholars have studied their significance as a separate entity. This has been especially in those cases in which families are bilingual, but live in non-bilingual societies, paying special attention to the language use patterns of the children. Lanza (2007) reports two main characteristics of **family bilingualism**. First, the **one person-one language** pattern (for instance, the father speaks in German and the mother speaks in French) is the most common family-interaction type that results in bilingualism. Second, parent's beliefs about bilingualism and languages are particularly relevant in the making of bilingual families.

MULTILINGUALISM

Families, schools and societies are not only instrumental in creating favourable conditions for bilingualism, but also for trilingualism and multilingualism. As with bilingualism, people might start the multilingual process through their closest environments such as their family. It is not uncommon that two parents speak two different languages to the children, and a third one is spoken at school. Another case is when the third language is learned through grandparents, caregivers or mass media. In many countries, families, schools and society are responsible for promoting multiple languages. For example, in Sweden three languages are usually spoken: Swedish, German and English. In many African countries and in India, individuals speak the local, regional and official languages. Elsewhere, three languages are spoken by the general population in Catalonia (Catalan, Spanish and English), Finland (Finish, Swedish and English) and Romani (Romanian, Hungarian and English).

Although research in early multilingualism is very limited (Paradis, 2007), scholars have identified some characteristics of multilingualism. **Passive multilingualism** is a characteristic found by scholars in the field. They have reported that in many cases one of the languages is understood, but rarely spoken by multilingual individuals. This aspect is connected to another feature: acceptance by peers. Multilingual individuals may stop using one language if that language is not viewed positively by their peers. Another significant feature of multilingualism is the role of codeswitching for effective communication. A case study reported by Dewaele (2000) shows that Livia, a young child who speaks French, Dutch, Urdu and English, uses code-switching to ensure that everyone can understand her requests. Finally, multilingualism is commonly developed sequentially and not simultaneously. In other words, multilinguals do not necessarily begin learning all of their languages from early in life; instead they continue learning languages throughout the lifespan.

Research on multilingualism is a growing area. Nowadays, this phenomenon is studied from different disciplines: sociolinguistic, psycholinguistic, sociology and psychology, among others. It is expected that this area of research will continue growing as does the multilingual population.

RELEVANCE TO EDUCATIONAL SETTINGS

Current thinking on how bilingualism is practiced encourages educators to promote children's first languages for many of the reasons outlined above. Moreover, the idea of keeping the two languages separate in the classroom is being challenged. For instance, codeswitching and translanguaging have been increasingly recognized as a growing reality for bilinguals and multilinguals, and as a potential pedagogical resource in the classroom (Creese and Blackledge, 2010; García, 2009). For instance, in the context of Africa and Asia, Van der Walt et al. (2001) advocate what they refer to as 'responsible codeswitching'. This entails using codeswitching to strengthen the connection to the home language and the content of what is being taught. At the same time, they state that most of classroom instruction needs to take place in the language that is being developed, whichever one that is. They also suggest that codeswitching needs to be meaningfully related to instructional support and not used in a random way, for instance, solely to provide orders or as a response to the language used by the child in a particular interaction in the classroom.

An example of translanguaging as a pedagogical resource is that of a secondary science class in the USA for Spanish-dominant students using a main text in English. The students have a text in Spanish to be used alongside the main (English) text, students write in both languages and the instructional exchange between teacher and students takes place mostly in Spanish (García, 2009). The two examples of using codeswitching and translanguaging in the classroom are described here because they underscore the recent understandings of bilingualism being (a) a resource, (b) more than the sum of two languages and (c) practiced in a way in which the two languages are not necessarily kept separate in instructional and family contexts – all points we have attempted to emphasize and promote in this chapter.

It is critical for educators to see the complexity involved in bilingual and multilingual children and adults using multiple languages. One is the necessity for teachers and administrators to see children as not necessarily having equivalent proficiency in two languages and to challenge the idealized view of the balanced bilingual. Rather, there is a need to view bilingual and multilingual children as using different languages in different ways, with different people and in different settings. Another necessary understanding is that bilingualism can be sequential or simultaneous. Therefore, the two languages need to be supported in different ways depending on the processes involved in people becoming bilingual. A last point for educators to remember is that when children are using both languages at the same time, it is not a sign of children being mixed up, but it is actually a sign of their command of both languages.

The difference between a person's academic and communicative proficiency in multiple languages is a critical distinction for educators to understand. In the USA, for instance, many children are moved out of language supportive environments, such as classrooms for English language learners, when they seem to have mastered a basic oral proficiency in a language, but they actually still need support to master the academic language. Much has been written about how to develop children's academic knowledge and use of language, and there is now an understanding that this actually involves ambitious pedagogies, time and support of the language-support teacher as well as the grade-level teacher. Last, it is critical to understand the role that schools and governments can have on bilingualism and multilingualism.

DISCUSSION AND REFLECTION QUESTIONS

1   Based on what you have read in this chapter, what would you say to a teacher who asked the parents of a student to give up the home language and instead use the school language at home?

2   What are the main benefits and challenges of raising bilingual/ multilingual children?

3   Provide some different examples of individual bilingualism and societal bilingualism. How are they linked to each other? How are they different from one another? What is needed to make an individual bilingual? What is needed to make a society bilingual?

RECOMMENDED READING AND VIEWING

A research-based guide about bilingual development in children written for parents and educators, see:
    Paradis, J., Genesee, F. and Crago, M. (2011), *Dual Language Development and Disorders* (2nd edn). Baltimore, MD: Paul H. Brookes.

For an accessible guide for parents to help their children become bilingual, see:
    King, K. A. and Mackey, A. (2007), *The Bilingual Edge: How, When and Why To Teach Your Child a Second Language*. New York, NY: HarperCollins.

For a fun book, based on research, which uses personal narratives to create positive bilingual environments, see:
    Pearson, B. Z. (2008), *Raising a Bilingual Child*. New York, NY: Living Language/Random House.

An article about the cognitive and physical benefits of bilingualism can be found at:
    www.guardian.co.uk/technology/2011/jun/12/ellen-bialystok-bilingual-brains-more-healthy

The TED talk by Patricia Kuhl, *The Linguistic Genius of Babies*, addresses the effectiveness of television in children learning languages:
www.ted.com/talks/patricia_kuhl_the_linguistic_genius_of_babies.html

For a useful website about raising bilingual children for parents and educators, see:
www.multilingualliving.com/about/

An accessible YouTube video about the benefits of knowing two languages can be found at:
www.youtube.com/watch?v=6Ye-BeVyJ5M&hl=en-GB&gl=SG&noredirect=1

9

How Does Policy Influence Language in Education?

Francis M. Hult

INTRODUCTION

When hearing the word 'policy', many people think first of lawmakers who draft and pass legislation and politicians who espouse platforms on various social issues, not teachers. Even with respect to educational policy, one might immediately call to mind national secretaries or ministers of education rather than educators. Teachers, however, are on the front line of language policy since the classroom is a key site where policies become action. Moreover, teachers make decisions every day that amount to developing language policies for their classrooms; for example, teachers decide which language(s) to use during instruction, which language(s) to encourage when students speak to each other, what words are taboo, etc. Policy, then, is not just an area that lawmakers and politicians should care about. In fact, a range of individuals are involved in making, interpreting, and implementing educational language policy other than legislators and education ministers: teachers, administrators, parents, textbook publishers, curriculum developers and the list goes on.

This chapter offers a glimpse into language policy with a particular focus on its relevance for educators. First, major considerations for language planning related to the domain of education are introduced. Then, I explore the different scales of society, ranging from governments to schools and classrooms, where educational policy and planning are shaped. Finally, the impact and relevance of language policy on educational settings is discussed with special attention to what teachers need to know.

PLANNING FOR LANGUAGES IN EDUCATION

Language policy, Spolsky (2004, p. 5) explains, includes a community's linguistic practices and beliefs about language as well as interventions to plan or change those practices and beliefs. A society may already have norms and expectations about how languages should be used and taught which have the effect of 'policy'. As such, they can be called **de facto language policies**. Alternatively, norms and expectations may be set forth in legal codes or documents as **de jure language policies** (Schiffman, 1996, p. 30). Language policy, then, involves efforts to plan or manage languages as well as how people think about and use languages. Thus, language policy goes hand in hand with language planning.

Types of planning

There are three central types of language planning: corpus planning, status planning and acquisition planning (Cooper, 1989). All three have relevance for the domain of education. **Corpus planning** deals with linguistic elements of a language such as standardizing grammar and spelling or developing vocabulary. **Status planning** addresses functional aspects of a language, for instance its role as a national language or medium of instruction in schools. **Acquisition planning**, in turn, relates to the allocation of resources and incentives to support individuals in learning a language.

While each of the three types of planning focus on different aspects of language in society, they are intertwined activities; effective policies and language planning efforts will account for all three. Furthermore, it may appear at first blush that only acquisition planning is related to education since it deals specifically with language learning; however, all three types, in fact, may be relevant to education. If, for instance, legislators in a particular country were to determine that an indigenous language should be used at all levels of education, it would (ideally) involve all three types of planning.

Status planning, which relates to language functions, might address questions such as these:

● Should certain schools and universities be designated as sites for indigenous language use or all of them?

- Which classrooms or subjects should use the indigenous language?

- When used, would the indigenous language be in bilingual distribution with (an)other language(s) or not?

Furthermore, in order for it to be possible to use the indigenous language for education in a wide range of subjects (see Chapter 8), there would also be corpus planning, which relates to language form, that might address these kinds of questions:

- Does the language need standardization for the purpose of creating and publishing materials and doing academic writing?

- What new vocabulary would need to be developed for specialized fields of study?

Then, there would be acquisition planning, which relates to language learning, with questions including:

- What training will be implemented to help teachers strengthen their competence in the indigenous language for academic purposes?

- What methods of instruction will be used to facilitate students' development of the indigenous language in tandem with other academic content?

- What economic, political or social incentives will there be for students to accept the learning and use of the indigenous language at different levels of education?

These are the kinds of issues that the Sámi University College in Norway has had to address. Bull (2012) explains that the primary mission of this university, which uses Sámi as a medium of instruction and administration, is to improve opportunities for the indigenous community, which previously did not have access to higher education in their own language. An explicit aim of the university is to develop Sámi as an academic language for science and research through collaboration and engagement with the indigenous community and its economic and cultural interests. As a practical example of the weight placed on language development, external board members are provided with Norwegian translation and interpretation so that Sámi can maintain a strong functional role as the primary language for the university setting.

Educational issues

Policy and planning, then, involve many practical issues about language in education. Medium of instruction choices are among the most central. These choices would include which language(s) should be used by teachers in the classroom and, by extension, be learned by students for academic purposes (Walter, 2008).

Decisions about medium of instruction are not necessarily made only on practical grounds. Structured English Immersion (SEI) in the state of Arizona (USA) is illustrative, as shown in a collection of studies assembled by Arias and Faltis (2012). During the first decade of the 2000s, the Arizona legislature engaged in a series of language policy and planning (LPP) activities that radically restricted the use of languages other than English in schools. Instead, they advanced SEI whereby English language learners are taught in English with limited language support. The language support, when provided, involves relatively inflexible progressions for teaching specific linguistic features. In developing the policy, many nuances in mainstream research about second language acquisition (SLA) were marginalized in favour of interpretations that supported lawmakers' beliefs about how additional languages are learned. In all, the educational language policy decisions strongly reflect ideologies about the status of English in the USA and negative attitudes towards multilingualism. The policy, in turn, has had far-reaching consequences on classroom teaching and teacher education. Many classroom teachers trained under previous policies have found themselves in the challenging position of navigating contradictions between current policy mandates and best practices accepted in the field of language teaching. Teachers educated in new teacher-training programs, focused mainly on the SEI techniques, run the risk of not learning those best practices for English language learners.

With respect to the education of the Deaf, *mode* of instruction takes on similar significance, as decisions need to be made about what role a sign language will play in the classroom vis-à-vis spoken language. These choices, too, may be made based on ideologies about deafness and not necessarily practical considerations or empirical evidence (Reagan, 2010). In the USA, for example, the dominant interpretation of educational policy is that the mainstream (i.e. oral) classroom is the least restrictive environment for students who are deaf because this setting allows for social integration with students and teachers who are not deaf. In mainstream classrooms, though, sign languages can sometimes become marginalized and opportunities for deaf students to develop high levels of academic proficiency in American Sign Language (ASL) can be reduced.

Sign language in these settings becomes a tool for academic support rather than a medium of instruction. Alternative interpretations of educational policy in the USA allow for educators to consider the communicative needs of deaf students, including whether or not those needs are best served in mainstream classrooms or in different settings together with other deaf students where sign language can be used as a medium of instruction thereby fostering advanced sign-language proficiency (Hult and Compton, 2012).

Languages that are not used for content instruction might nonetheless be included in the educational domain. One part of making language policy would be to decide which of these languages will be taught as subjects, whether they will be optional or required, and how much instructional time they will be allotted. Like medium of instruction choices, the distribution of additional languages in educational curricula is sometimes based on ideology and politics and not merely on student/parent demand or practical communication needs. In the Swedish national curricula, for instance, the Swedish and English languages are designated as required core subjects alongside content areas like math and science. The Swedish language has this status by virtue of its position as the national language of Sweden. English, which has been part of the Swedish educational system in some form since the nineteenth century, is set apart from other modern languages like French and German because of values held in Swedish society about the role of English for internationalization (Cabau-Lampa, 2007; Hult, 2012).

Once decisions are in place about which languages will serve as media of instruction and/or as subjects, decisions about evaluation need to be taken into account as well. When a new student begins school, how will it be determined if she or he has the requisite competence in the medium of instruction or if some kind of additional instruction in that language is needed? For example, if a new student comes from Somalia to a school in Stockholm where Swedish is the medium of instruction, how will it be determined if the student has the necessary language skills for content learning? What if the student does not (which is likely)? If she or he needs additional instruction, how will it be determined when the necessary competence has been achieved? With respect to languages as subjects, will there be assessments to determine achievement and readiness to go on to a higher level? If a language is a required subject, will students be asked to demonstrate a certain level of ability, and, if so, how will that be evaluated? Indeed, since they serve as gatekeeping devices, language assessments (and even general educational assessments that assume specific linguistic skills) themselves act as language policies since they are used to determine students' educational opportunities (Menken, 2008).

In addition to evaluation, other pedagogical factors might also be included in language policies. With respect to acquisition planning, for instance, policies might prescribe the teaching methods to be used in instruction as well as desired outcomes from such instruction. As a critical practitioner or policy analyst, one might carefully examine such prescriptions to determine the extent to which they match current empirical evidence from SLA research. For example, Whitney (2012) found that United States refugee education policy specifies as few as 80 hours for English language learning before newcomers are expected to seek employment whereas SLA research suggests that as long as two to three years may be needed for students to develop strong proficiency for everyday communication. Even decisions that might seem only administrative at first can actually be about language pedagogy, such as budgetary choices about providing (or not) funds to hire teachers, buy textbooks or provide supplies since they are likely to affect students' language development.

What should be included in language education policies is an important question because education, as a vital social institution, plays a special role in the linguistic development of children and young adults. In many places around the world, regulations have been set forth in governmental documents that establish specific **language rights**, or legal rights related to the use and learning of specific languages. For instance, the European Charter for Regional or Minority Languages, a Council of Europe treaty, is a well-known example of a policy that guides governments in setting forth rights for certain linguistic minorities in education and other domains of society.

Skutnabb-Kangas (2000, p. 502) argues that certain rights to language in education are so fundamental that they should be considered among a person's **linguistic human rights**. These include:

- to identify with one's mother tongue,
- to learn and develop one's mother tongue in all modalities,
- to receive education through the medium of one's mother tongue,
- to become bi/trilingual in one's mother tongue and an official language when they are different, and
- to benefit from education regardless of one's mother tongue.

Language rights, including linguistic human rights, have not been without controversy, and they continue to form part of political and intellectual debates in countries around the world. Edwards (2008), for example, points out that government policies outlining language rights can amount to little more than empty declarations when no clear actions are specified for what the rights mean in practice. It is also possible in some cases, as Skutnabb-Kangas has pointed out, that policies are written in vague ways that allow governments to provide only minimal, if any, support and protection for linguistic minorities when they find it economically or politically challenging to do so.

At the same time, language rights in legislation do offer legal avenues for linguistic minorities to assert those rights. There have been many well-known legal cases around the world that have had major effects on education. One such example is the *Lau* v. *Nichols* case that was heard by the Supreme Court of the United States in 1974. The court found that simply providing students with the same access to schools, texts and teachers did not amount to equal treatment when students do not have the linguistic ability to understand what they are being taught. The result was what became known as the 'Lau remedies', which specified that students who are not proficient in English cannot be expected to access education in English without support such as English as a second language instruction or bilingual education. This case is also notable because it is an example of how legislation not originally designed to address language issues can be used to leverage language rights. The Lau case was built upon *civil* rights to non-discrimination and equal protection under law that are not specifically about language. Language became an issue because of its importance to educational access. It is a good illustration of why teachers need to be aware of any law or policy that could have an effect on their students.

Policies and legal frameworks, though, are not absolute guarantees of educational equity for linguistic minorities. Since policies and laws are open to interpretation, it is possible for officials to read them narrowly or use them to advance their own points of view. One could ask, for example, whether or not the decisions to limit resources and support for English language learners in Arizona, as discussed earlier, actually violate the guidelines that emerged from the Lau case.

SCALES OF POLICY AND PLANNING

As the discussion thus far might suggest, Language policy and planning (LPP) takes place on multiple scales of society. Some examples of these scales are noted in Table 9.1.

TABLE 9.1 Social scales for LPP

Supra-/international organizations and governments
National/regional governments
Special groups/organizations (e.g. language academies)
Corporations
Social/religious institutions (e.g. schools)
→ Individuals

The role of institutions

It is easy to see the connections between LPP and some of the examples in Table 9.1. Policies are readily associated with (quasi-) governmental bodies such as the supranational European Union, Council of Europe or African Union; the national governments of sovereign states; and the regional governments of provinces within states. In addition, though, LPP efforts may take shape in other settings.

There are special organizations, sometimes governmental and sometimes not, that have unique responsibilities for LPP such as the Académie française in France, the Real Academia Española in Spain and the National Languages Committee in Taiwan, among many others around the globe. There is even the Klingon Language Institute (www.kli.org/) for the constructed language popularized by the *Star Trek* television programs and films. Language academies engage in a variety of language planning tasks, often related to linguistic form (corpus planning). In Sweden, *Svenska Akademien*, in its continuing corpus planning work, periodically publishes a list of words it officially considers to belong to the Swedish language: *Svenska Akademiens ordlista over svenska språket*. It also publishes grammar books. In most cases, institutions such as these do not make language laws, but their standardization of languages through dictionaries, grammar books and word lists do govern the very nature of legitimized language and has direct consequences for education by virtue of prescribing what forms of a language should be taught and the norms against which students should be measured. In the absence of formal language academies, as is the case for American English, major publishers that produce grammar texts and dictionaries serve a similar function in practice.

Other organizations might also play roles in LPP which can have residual impacts on education. Major multinational corporations have offices in countries throughout the world and some create policies for what the internal working language(s) will be, whether the national language of its headquarters offices, local languages or a language of wider communication. Hiring criteria for these corporations, particularly at higher levels, may include specific language abilities thus creating incentives to learn new languages among those who aspire to a career with such a company. Widespread corporate expectations for proficiency in a language of wider communication, like English, can reinforce local values about the importance of that language in a national education system (Berg et al., 2001).

The use of languages for religious purposes is also well documented as having an effect on language acquisition. The relationship between Hebrew with Judaism and Arabic with Islam are two well-known examples. The religious affiliation contributes significantly to the learning of these languages on a global scale, including in societies where they might not otherwise be widely used. These languages take on deep significance and serve specific sacred functions in these societies. In other cases, religious institutions may serve to strengthen a cultural, even if not sacred, connection to a language. Churches that serve immigrant communities may offer weekend language courses so that first- and second-generation children may continue to develop, or in some cases reclaim, their heritage languages. In other cases, churches sometimes offer language classes to immigrants in the dominant language of a society as a type of social and religious outreach.

Educational institutions, of course, are central to LPP efforts related to language learning and development. Here, too, there may be multiple scales involved, depending on administrative organization. In the USA, state (i.e. provincial) legislatures make laws governing education in their respective states. Within each state there are also state departments of education, municipal school districts and individual schools. All of these, in turn, are guided by national laws and guidelines regarding education and the allocation of federal funds. On each of these different scales, there might be specific policy documents, some with the force of law and some functioning as guidelines for implementation, that govern how education should take place. Decisions about the previously discussed issues like medium of instruction, allocation of material and human resources and assessment are set forth in these policies.

The role of individuals

The different scales discussed thus far should not be seen as existing in purely hierarchical or linear relationships, but as operating in different, albeit interconnected, spheres of society. In some cases, the policy implementation ideal is a linear one (e.g. supranational organization → national government → regional government → schools → individuals). However, it must be recognized that individuals on each scale (re)interpret policies and shape them rather than serve as policy automatons (Shohamy, 2006). In this sense, as the arrow in Table 9.1 suggests, the individual is not like the other scales. While policy and planning might be done on an individual scale, like a parent making a family language policy, individuals also make decisions within all of the other scales. In fact, it is individual interpretation of policy that allows for agency, creativity and the opportunity to seek out what Hornberger (2002) terms **implementational space**: areas in language policies that can be leveraged or exploited to promote multilingual education. (See Johnson, 2011, for further discussion.) In her research on language education for deaf students in the State of Texas, Compton (2010) found that key individuals on state, district and school scales interpreted policies by drawing on their own beliefs about deafness and sign language. Sometimes an individual educator made a narrow interpretation of policies from other scales that potentially reduced implementational space for the use of ASL in the classroom while in other instances different individuals made broader interpretations that expanded implementational space.

Language policy implementation, thus, is not always linear and not always top-down. Individual educators play a key role in LPP. In some countries, like Sweden, educators are encouraged at school and classroom scales to interpret national curricula directly. In other countries, like the USA, policy interpretations are often further mediated as state department of education officials offer policy interpretations to school district administrators who then offer policy interpretations to teacher supervisors who then offer policy interpretations to teachers who then offer policy interpretations to their students by accepting or resisting these other various interpretations when teaching. At each phase, there is room for agency as individuals draw upon their training, experiences, beliefs and ideas from other scales noted in Table 9.1 in ways that may be non-linear. For example, a teacher who has carefully read state educational policy which allows for the use of two languages in school might leverage that knowledge to resist a district policy which recommends English-only in the classroom. In this way, the teacher can open implementational space for bilingual instruction in the classroom. Alternatively, a district administrator with a negative attitude towards a particular minority language might interpret state policy in an exceedingly narrow way in an attempt to close implementational space for bilingual instruction.

The role of individuals in LPP processes is not limited to educational institutions. While policies are frequently given invisible authority as texts, it is important to recognize that they are, in fact, negotiated and written by individuals (Ball, 2006; Hult, 2010a). As such, Wiley (1996, p. 109) suggests, it is useful to ask 'Who defines language problems? How do they become problems? For whom are they a problem? And, perhaps most important, does language planning itself ever cause language and communication problems?' Just like educators, lawmakers are guided by their training, experiences, beliefs and ideas that might come from various social scales shown in Table 9.1.

As we saw in the Arizona situation discussed earlier, language issues that become concerns for educational policy are not neutral nor are the solutions that are devised and written into policy documents. In her study of the development of the No Child Left Behind policy in the USA, Woodson (2010) showed that the language ideologies and beliefs about language learning held by senators and congressional representatives heavily influenced the mandates that were set forth in the final policy text.

In some cases, even with good intentions, policy mandates can cause harm to the very individuals they are intended to help. The negative impact on the academic achievement of English language learners in the wake of the No Child Left Behind policy in the USA is a quintessential example. Demands for educational testing that were meant to focus students and teachers on achieving high standards, for instance, instead became barriers to success because the policy did not adequately take into account the linguistic challenges English language learners face in the classroom (Menken, 2008).

While the motivations of individual policymakers might be useful to know, it may not always be possible or practical to determine exactly what they are. A critical reader of policy can, however, ascertain specific orientations to language that offer a window into the spirit of a policy: language-as-problem, language-as-resource and language-as-right (Ruíz, 1984). It is possible, if not likely, that more than one of these orientations will appear in a single policy.

A **language-as-problem** orientation frames a language issue that needs to be fixed, and it may even position a particular group of speakers as presenting a challenge. In a policy that aims to transition students from using their mother tongue to instead using a dominant language, the existing linguistic abilities of those students are problematized and undervalued. In contrast, a **language-as-resource** orientation positions students' existing linguistic abilities in a positive way, highlighting their applicability to accessing opportunities for learning and social engagement. A policy that promotes developmental bilingualism throughout a student's educational career and/or emphasizes the social, psychological and economic opportunities that come with a broad linguistic repertoire values languages as resources. Finally, a **language-as-right** orientation emphasizes that students have legal rights with respect to language learning and development. This orientation relates to the earlier discussion about language rights and linguistic human rights such as whether or not education is provided in the medium of a student's mother tongue. In contrast to the ideals of linguistic human rights, those linguistic rights which are considered essential to human dignity, there are many language (education) laws around the world that are merely permissive of multilingualism or even restrict it, as in Arizona. Educators need to be critical readers of policy in order to know what orientations to language are taken in policies that affect their students.

ECOLOGY OF LANGUAGE POLICY

It should be clear by now that LPP is multidimensional and involves interconnections among a wide range of contexts and individuals. With this in mind, we can use the metaphor of 'ecology' to understand it. Just as the usual meaning of ecology relates to interconnections in our natural environment, **language ecology** is useful in understanding and articulating interrelationships among languages in LPP.

Haugen (1972) suggests that it is fruitful to focus on *relationships* among languages in both sociological and psychological ways. When investigating a language in social context, Haugen remarks, one should attend to 'its interaction with other languages in the minds of bi- and multilingual speakers' and to 'its interaction with the society in which it functions as a medium of communication' (p. 325). Language ecology, in this way, emphasizes the full range of scales involved in LPP as shown in Table 9.1: international, national, regional, local and individual.

While language ecology relates to all aspects of multilingualism in society, it has been identified as useful for conceptualizing multidimensional aspects of language policy, in particular. As such, it can help teachers figure out what a policy situation looks like and how it affects them. Hornberger and Hult (2008, p. 285) set forth a series of specific questions that serve as a guide to engaging with language policy in its social context:

Three general information-gathering questions:

- How are relationships among different languages reflected in policy documents?

- How do language policies relate to individual experiences with language use and beliefs about language(s)?

- How do language policies relate to sociolinguistic circumstances 'on the ground'?

And two general critical thinking questions:

- How do language policies at multiple levels of social organization interact?
- Do policies promote equitable multilingualism?

These questions, while also useful for LPP researchers, are helpful for educational practitioners to explore and reflect upon the policy landscape in which they work. (Readers interested in using these questions to guide language policy research should see Hult, 2010a.)

A first step in exploring a language policy landscape is to identify the policies. These might be legislative texts or curricular documents. They might be written as language policies, for example specifying a national language, or they might be crafted as general educational policies that have direct implications for language learners. For example, educational policies about content assessment that assume testing will take place in a dominant language become, in practice, language policies because they assume achievement of the level of language proficiency needed to take the test. Accordingly, when seeking out policies, it is important to look broadly for the documents that apply to a particular educational context and determine which ones are being used to guide and inform practice. These might be documents which one would not normally think of as 'policy' such as school handbooks or even official websites when they are used to normalize pedagogical activities, practices or beliefs.

It should be kept in mind that the kinds of policy and planning considerations described thus far might not always be overt and explicit, that is to say clearly articulated or appear in published documents. They might be covert, as in situations where teachers' or administrators' normalized behaviours around language in education run counter to published, overt policies (Schiffman, 1996, p. 13). For example, teachers at a school might decide to provide bilingual instruction even though a state's official policy calls for monolingual instruction in a dominant national language. Policies might also be implicit, emerging more by virtue of norms and practices established over time than explicitly stated either orally or in writing. Even in the absence of any official policy, decisions are being made. As Fishman has pointed out, '"no policy" leaves whatever language is "in control" still in the "driver's seat" and, therefore, a "no policy" policy . . . is always a silent vote for the continuation of the status quo and of those who benefit thereby' (2006, p. 125).

With policies identified, the first three ecological questions provide a guide to information gathering. The first question suggests that one should consider how languages are positioned in relation to each other. Policies might present certain languages as more useful or important than others or they might attempt to promote equality among different languages. Some languages might be absent completely such that their relationship to other languages is rendered invisible in policies. The first question, then, highlights how power relationships and linguistic hierarchies are written into the text.

The second question involves connecting policies to people, as in the earlier discussion about the role of individuals in policy processes. How policies are written will depend on the experiences and beliefs about language that are held by policymakers. Similarly, how policies are interpreted and implemented will depend upon the experiences and beliefs about language that are held by educational administrators and teachers. There might be differences between policy objectives and beliefs on the ground when, for example, strongly held language attitudes about the value of a minority language clash with a policy designed to promote the use of that minority language in educational contexts.

The third question is sociological in nature, encompassing issues related to how a policy as written matches the ways in which language and linguistic resources are used in practice. Effective policies tend to align with lived sociolinguistic circumstances (Schiffman, 1996, p. 49). It might be difficult to implement a monolingual policy in a linguistically diverse community because it contradicts how teachers and students use language in their daily lives. Such a policy might be overtly resisted or ignored in practice as individuals use language as they ordinarily would. It might also lead to educational failure when policies set up unrealistic demands on student attainment in the medium of an additional language.

The second set of questions offer ways to think critically and analytically about policies. The first of these focuses on the multiple scales shown in Table 9.1. Policies on multiple scales might or might not be purposefully designed to interact. Decisions made by a language academy, such as codifying a grammar, might be made for ostensibly intellectual or aesthetic reasons without necessarily incurring legal obligations on the part of schools to follow those standards. Nonetheless, the social value placed on a language academy's decisions can be so strong that schools will voluntarily abide by them. In contrast, national education law can place legal obligations on provinces or states, and provincial or state law, in turn, can place legal obligations on districts and schools. Policies across these scales are often written in dialogue with each other. One policy might be explicitly cited or quoted in another or ideas in one policy might be invoked in another in more implicit ways. Even still, there is no guarantee that such policies will be in lockstep with each other. There might be contradictions or conflicts across policies on different scales since policymakers have different beliefs and interpretations of policy discourses and educational circumstances. Navigating these contradictions and conflicts is one way to seek out the implementational spaces mentioned earlier.

The second critical thinking question is an evaluative one. With an understanding of how policies are framed and languages are positioned within and across them, a critical evaluation can lift forward whether or not policies are favourable towards multilingualism and educational opportunities for all students regardless of language. It might not always be possible for all languages in a particular community to be part of a structured curriculum, either as a medium of instruction or as a subject, but that does not mean they should be ignored. The languages that students already know and use can serve as resources to support their content learning and additional language development (see Chapter 8).

Using and valuing multilingualism is a way of communicating to children and their parents that their linguistic resources have social capital, that is to say value and importance in society. We can carefully read educational language policies, including curricula, to determine whether or not they provide guidance on how students' existing linguistic skills should be used in the classroom. In addition, a critical reading of policy should include a view towards how different languages are treated with respect to the wide range of concerns noted in the earlier section on educational issues. Inequitable policies add to circumstances that can lead to language endangerment or loss.

RELEVANCE TO EDUCATIONAL SETTINGS

Policy is intimately related to education, affecting all aspects of it from national configurations of educational systems to the very actions that teachers take during interaction with their students. As such, it is of high importance to all stakeholders: legislators, administrators, teachers, students, parents and community members at large. What is included (or not included) in policy directly influences people's lives.

With respect to educational practice, there are both direct and indirect effects of policy (Hult, 2010b, p. 23). Practice might be indirectly influenced by decisions such as the allocation of material, financial and human resources. While these are not directly pedagogical decisions, they have consequences for what teachers can accomplish in practice. Class sizes that come about due to the funding allocated for hiring teachers with multilingual skills, for instance, will shape interactional opportunities in the classroom. Priority levels set for bi-/multilingual library materials will shape what teachers have access to and can integrate in their teaching. More directly, policies sometimes include provisions specifically about pedagogy such as what percentage of which languages are permitted for instruction, which assessments to administer and to whom, which textbooks are to be used and the topics to be covered.

Since educational language policy is ultimately enacted and implemented in schools and classrooms, educators are the policy 'arbiters' (Menken and García, 2010, p. 1) who interpret, implement and potentially resist or subvert policy to meet students' needs on a daily basis. The more knowledgeable educators are about policies, the better they are at navigating them and claiming agency when enacting them. By directly engaging with policies themselves, rather than receiving second-hand interpretations and directives from supervisors, educators can most effectively seek out implementational spaces for the pedagogical creativity needed to best serve their students.

In sum, then, here are some basics about what teachers need to know about language policy:

- Classrooms are spaces where multilingualism and politics intersect; teaching is not an apolitical act.

- What the policies actually are (whether implicit/explicit, unofficial/ official, local/regional/national); read them first-hand.

- Teachers play a crucial role in implementing policy as well as in making their own classroom policies.

- Teachers have agency in interpreting policies, whether to enact them creatively or to subvert them.

- Actively making connections between policies and pedagogy is a central part of teaching.

DISCUSSION AND REFLECTION QUESTIONS

1   What counts as a 'policy' in your teaching/learning context? Try to think of at least one example of an implicit or unofficial (*de facto*) policy and one example of an explicit or official (*de jure*) policy? With these examples in mind, consider why a *de facto* policy might influence educational practice as much, if not more, than a *de jure* policy?

2   If policies are open to negotiation and interpretation by individuals on multiple scales of society (e.g. national educational agencies, state departments of education, school districts and classrooms), what is

the purpose of making policies in the first place? Why not simply let people make individual decisions on their own?

3   Should teachers resist or subvert a policy when it contradicts their professional expertise about what is pedagogically appropriate for their students? If not, why? If so, how should they do it? What risks and consequences might be involved?

RECOMMENDED READING AND VIEWING

Corson's *Language Policy in Schools* (1999) is written specifically with the educator in mind. It provides practical hands-on advice for engaging with current policy and also making new language policies for schools. See Chapter 8, in particular, for a series of in-depth questions to consider.

Corson, D. (1999), *Language Policy in Schools: A Resource for Teachers and Administrators*. London: Routledge.

You will find an extended discussion of many of the issues taken up in the present chapter in Johnson (2013). While it deals with language policy in general, educational language policy features prominently as well. It is an excellent next step for a reader who would like to dig deeper into language policy issues.

Johnson, D. C. (2013), *Language Policy*. New York, NY: Palgrave Macmillan.

For readers who would like to delve further into specific issues and challenges related to educational language policy, Tollefson (2013) provides empirical and theoretical insight with examples from contexts around the world.

Tollefson, J. W. (2013), *Language Policies in Education: Critical Issues* (2nd edn). London: Routledge.

Glossary

Academic language Language that is used in educational contexts and for educational purposes. Academic language is often more grammatically complex than conversation in daily life, with a greater variety of vocabulary as well as vocabulary specific to particular disciplines.

Accent A way of pronouncing the set of **phonemes** (speech sounds) of a language. All languages can be spoken with several accents. It is impossible to speak a language without using an accent.

Accommodation A term developed by Howard Giles to refer to the tendency of speakers in a friendly situation to converge in **linguistic form**.

Acquisition planning Language planning that relates to the allocation of resources and incentives to support individuals in learning a language.

Acts of Identity A term developed by R. B. Le Page to refer to the use of specific **linguistic forms** by speakers hoping to express aspects of their identity to their hearers.

Additive bilingualism Maintenance of the home language while the second, school or societal language is learned.

Affix A meaningful component (in word formation) which cannot stand alone as a word, for example *un-* as in *unusual,* or *-ly* as in *usually.*

Affixation The process of adding an **affix** in word formation; contrasted with **compounding**.

Ambiguity When something that is said or written has two or more different meanings, whether or not intended by the user.

Antonyms Words with opposite meanings.

Asymmetrical classroom talk Classroom talk is considered to be 'asymmetrical' in that the teacher usually talks more, has control over the topic and of who is allowed to talk. Thus, it is asymmetrical not only in quantity but also in terms of who has authority over the talk.

Babbling Babies' first productions of language-like sounds, consisting of repetitive consonant-vowel sequences (e.g. *bababa*).

Balanced bilingual Refers to someone who has equal control in two languages. This is an idealized term that theoretically has been useful to do research; however, it is problematic when it is used to categorize people.

Basic interpersonal communication skills (BICS) Ability of language minority children to speak fluently in informal contexts.

Case The different forms a noun or **pronoun** takes depending on its grammatical function in a phrase or sentence. In English, only pronouns have case.

Child-directed speech (CDS) (Also called 'motherese' or 'caregiver speech') A speech **style** often adopted in interactions with young children, characterized by exaggerated intonation, short and repetitive **utterances** and generally positive affect.

Choice questions Based on work by Mehan (1979), choice questions are those that offer the respondent a choice. This might be yes/no, either/or or a choice from a limited set of options.

Code A way of speaking or writing. This is an open term that can be used to refer to different varieties of a language, or to different languages.

Codeswitching Refers to those situations in which individuals switch between one or more languages, varieties or codes in the context of a single conversation.

Cognitive academic language proficiency (CALP) The academic language which is developed within schooling and **literacy** contexts.

Cognitive benefits Advantages of being bilingual related to the brain and mind.

Coherence Connection achieved by relating a stretch of language to the context when interpreting it as a **text** that makes sense.

Cohesion Connections or links that exist in a stretch of language and hold the stretch of language together. Cohesion helps to identify a stretch of language as a **text**.

Common Underlying Proficiency (CUP) Explains that the two languages for bilinguals are not stored separately but that there is a common underlying linguistic proficiency.

Communicative signal Behaviour that is used purposefully to relay information.

Compounding The joining of two or more words to produce a different word (in contrast with **affixation**),

for example joining *sing* and *song* to produce *singsong*.

Conjunction A grammatical term for words which link sentences or clauses together and indicate temporal, spatial, causal or logical relationships between the sentences or clauses.

Contingent speech A comment on or a response made by an adult to a topic introduced by a child in order to extend the conversation.

Corpus planning Language planning that deals with linguistic elements of a language such as standardizing grammar and spelling or developing vocabulary.

Criterial A term used in **identity sociolinguistics**, developed by Anthea Fraser Gupta. A criterial feature is a grammatical form of high frequency (such as a BE deletion) which characterizes a particular **dialect** for its speakers and which can be used in quantificational studies of dialectal **codeswitching**. See also **emblematic**, **indexical**, **stylization**.

Critical period A limited window of time in language development during which exposure to certain linguistic stimuli is necessary for language to be learned.

Cumulative talk Based on work by Mercer (2002), cumulative talk encourages students to build on each other's responses in ways that are positive and with little criticism.

De facto language policies Norms and expectations about how languages should be used and taught which have the effect of policy while not being officially specified in a text.

De jure language policies Norms and expectations about how languages should be used and taught as set forth in legal codes or documents.

Decontextualized (oral) language Language used to convey information about things, people, etc. which are not in the immediate environment of the speaker and the hearer or for audiences who may share only limited amounts of background knowledge with the speaker.

Deictic items Linguistic elements that are used to point to people, objects, places, etc. during an interaction, for example *this*, *that*, *there*.

Derivation A subtype of **affixation** (in contrast with **inflection**) in which an **affix** is added to a word to produce a different word, for example adding -*er* to *sing*, to produce *singer*.

Dialect Used in a number of different ways in linguistics. It is most usually defined as a regional variety of a language that differs in terms of accent, words and grammar.

Dialectologist A person who studies **dialects**.

Dialectology The study of **dialects**.

Dialogic teaching Promoted especially by Alexander (2008), this is an overall approach to teaching, not a teaching strategy. It is intended to encourage open-ended discussion among students to explore issues, problems and student thinking.

Diglossia The situation in which two languages coexist in the same society for different purposes/uses. Ferguson (1959) defined this as a separation of High and Low varieties.

Diphthong A kind of vowel where the tongue moves from one position to another, thus producing a glide as in the pronunciation of *out* and *toy* (in contrast with **monophthong**).

Disciplinary literacy The ability to use the language of the disciplines effectively and fluently. Thus, for example, learning history is as much about learning to talk, read and write history as it is about learning the facts, issues and processes that constitute history.

Discourse A term used to describe language in use and how the purposes, participants, environments, processes, etc. of interactions play a role in the construction of **texts**.

Discourse community A group of people with a suitable degree of professional expertise who share goals and purposes, and who communicate with each other to achieve those goals (Swales, 1990).

Display questions These are questions intended to encourage students to 'display' their knowledge. They are more frequently present in classroom talk (as compared with daily conversations) because teachers often ask questions to which they know the answer, only because they want to encourage students to display what they know/have learned.

Disputational talk Based on work by Mercer (2002), this is talk characterized by individualized thinking in which disagreements, assertions and challenges are present.

Dominant language Describes the language that a bilingual would consider to be more proficient in.

Elitist bilingualism Refers to those situations in which parents from a high socio-economic status, without living in a bilingual society, decide to enroll their children in bilinguals program.

Ellipsis Omission of some elements, such as a noun or a clause, in a sentence structure.

Emblematic As used in **identity sociolinguistics**, a linguistic form (such as a word, or a particular pronunciation) that acts as a badge for a particular group of people. See also **indexical**, **criterial**, **stylization**.

Executive control Part of human cognition and information processing ability which helps to manage attention especially when tasks compete for attention or resolving conflicts with different information inputs. See www2. psychology.uiowa.edu/faculty/ hazeltine//executivecontrol.html for a general explanation (not specifically related to language).

Exploratory talk Based on work by Mercer (2002), exploratory talk is talk in which students explore ideas or work through emerging ideas. It might be characterized by hesitations and tentativeness as students are still developing the ideas they are working towards.

Family bilingualism Refers to those situations in which the members of a family speak two languages, usually in a monolingual society.

First language acquisition Acquiring a first language in life, in naturalistic settings. Note that this might involve more than one language, for example, bilinguals who begin acquiring two or more languages at home from early in life. See also **second language acquisition** and **second language learning**.

Foreign language learning Studying a language that is not your home language and in a social context in which that language is not commonly used (e.g. studying Portuguese in India).

Genres Ways of achieving distinct social purposes through the use of particular language forms.

Grammatical cohesion Links established through the use of grammatical features such as **pronouns** and **conjunctions**.

Grammatical function The different roles of the components of a structure, for example in *The cat vomited*, the component *the cat* is the Subject, while the component *vomited* has the function, Verb.

Hyponyms The meaning of one word represents a member of a class represented by the meaning of the other word, for example the word *parrot* is a hyponym of the word *bird*.

Identity sociolinguistics An approach to **sociolinguistics** that focuses on the speakers' active projection of identity on a particular occasion.

Implementational space Areas in language policies that can be leveraged or exploited to promote multilingual education.

Indexical A term used in **identity sociolinguistics**, developed by Michael Silverstein and Penelope Eckert (see Eckert, 2008). An indexical feature is a **linguistic form** (such as a word, or a particular pronunciation) that in a particular context is associated with a group of social characteristics (an indexical field). See also **emblematic**, **criterial**, **stylization**.

Inferences Knowledge and information about the world drawn on by the listener or reader to create connections and arrive at interpretations which are not actually expressed by the words.

Inflection A subtype of affixation (in contrast with **derivation**) in which an **affix** is added to a word to produce a variant form of the same word, for example adding /-s/ to *sing*, to produce *sings*.

Interlanguage A term used to refer to a learner's developing second language, emphasizing that although it may differ from the target language as spoken by native speakers, it is an internally consistent linguistic system.

International Phonetic Alphabet (IPA) The most commonly used universal alphabet for representing speech sounds in human languages. See www.langsci.ucl.ac.uk/ipa/

IRF/IRE A well-established sequence of teacher-student talk in classrooms. This usually includes a three-part structure: Initiate-Respond-Evaluate (IRE) or Initiate-Respond-Feedback (IRF). The teacher initiates so that students can respond and the teacher can then evaluate/provide feedback.

Labovian sociolinguistics Same as **variationist sociolinguistics**. This term emphasizes the importance of the founder William Labov in establishing a theory and a methodology.

Language awareness Explicit knowledge about and awareness of language. See also the website of the Association for Language Awareness (www.lexically.net/ala/la_defined.htm).

Language ecology A metaphor that draws upon ideas from environmental ecology to understand and articulate interrelationships between languages and speakers of languages.

Language instruction The teaching or instruction of language as an object of study (e.g. teaching Chinese, English, Spanish).

Language policy The codification of a community's linguistic practices as well as interventions to plan or change those practices.

Language rights Legal rights related to the use and learning of specific languages.

Language-as-problem An orientation to language (policy) that frames a language issue as needing to be fixed, and may even position a particular group of speakers as presenting a challenge.

Language-as-resource An orientation to language (policy) that positions students' existing linguistic abilities in a positive way, highlighting their applicability to accessing opportunities for learning and social engagement.

Language-as-right An orientation to language (policy) that emphasizes legal rights with respect to language learning and development.

Lexical ambiguity When **ambiguity** arises from the various meanings of one (or more) of the words in the sentence.

Lexical cohesion Links created through the repetition of words or the use of words which are related in meanings in a stretch of language.

Lexical density The ratio of content words to function words in relation to the total length of a clause or a sentence.

Linguistic forms Any meaningful units of language (e.g. morphemes, words, phrases, etc.).

Linguistic human rights Fundamental language rights that are considered essential to human dignity.

Linguistic inquiry A systematic exploration of language data.

Linguistic interdependence hypothesis The hypothesis suggests that language and **literacy** skills can be transferred from L1 to L2 in bilingual learners. It indicates that some reading skills are basic and fundamental in the reading process; therefore, once such skills are learned in one language, these can be used in any other language.

Linguistic variable In **Labovian sociolinguistics**, a linguistic feature that varies within a particular community without changing the referential meaning of what is said. Linguistic variables are written in round brackets.

Linguistic variant In **Labovian sociolinguistics**, one of the specific forms of a **linguistic variable** in a particular community.

Linguistic variation Difference in form within a language. There can be linguistic variation in any aspect of language, such as grammar, words or pronunciation.

Linguistics The study of language.

Literacy The development of reading and writing skills in formal, informal and academic contexts.

Majority language The language that is considered of higher status and more powerful in a particular context or country.

Mean length of utterance (MLU) A measure of grammatical development, indexed by the average number of morphemes per **utterance** in a child/learner's speech.

Medium of instruction The language or 'medium' used for teaching in schools (e.g. Japanese in Japanese schools). In a bilingual (or trilingual) education system, there might be more than one medium of instruction.

Meronyms The meaning of one word denotes a constituent part of something denoted by the meaning of the other word, for example the word *wheel* is a meronym of the word *car*.

Metalanguage The technical language needed to talk about language as a subject matter.

Metaprocess questions Based on work by Mehan (1979), metaprocess questions are those which address students' knowledge processes, for example *How do you know that?*

Minority language The language that is considered of lower status and not as powerful in a particular context or country.

Monophthong A kind of vowel sound produced with the tongue in a single position as in the pronunciation of *odd* and *think* (in contrast with **diphthong**).

Morpheme The smallest component of a word, for example *teacher* can be analysed as consisting of two morphemes, *teach + -er*.

Morphology The study of word formation – how **morphemes** are put together to form words.

Multimodal More than one mode or channel of communication used in a single text.

Nominalization The process of changing verbs, adjectives or adverbs in a clause into nouns for things and abstract concepts, a feature commonly found in formal writing.

Non-fluency features A characteristic of spontaneous spoken interaction which breaks the flow of speech (e.g. fillers *er, umm* and false start such as, *they they com- they know that . . .*).

One person-one language A way for parents to separate the teaching of two languages to their children.

Onomatopoeic words Words that resemble the sounds or action they describe.

Oracy The use of speaking and listening skills to communicate effectively and influence the social world, including using talk to learn and construct knowledge jointly with others.

Orientation The setting of a story that introduces the characters, the time and the place where the event occurs.

Overextension A child's use of a *word* with a meaning that is too general (e.g. *dog* = any four-legged animal). See **underextension.**

Overgeneralization The application of a *rule* in a context where it would be predicted to apply, but does not (e.g. English past tense formation: *go+ed* = *goed*, yet should be *went*).

Passive multilingualism Describes those individuals who can understand several languages but do not speak all those languages.

Phoneme A central concept in phonetics. A phoneme is a speech sound and is part of the structure of pronunciation in a language. For example, in most accents of English, the phoneme /k/ begins *keep, cool* and *clean*, and is also found in *skin, sink* and *lock*. The precise (phonetic) pronunciation of the /k/ is different in these six contexts. There are other languages in which, for example, the /k/ of *keep* and the /k/ of *skin* are different phonemes.

Phonetics The study of speech sounds.

Pragmatic competence The ability to use language effectively to fulfil communicative functions and goals.

Presentational talk Based on work by Barnes (1992), this is talk which is used to demonstrate, rather than develop understanding, to show or present what is known.

Problem (in a narrative) A complication in a story which needs to be resolved. See also **resolution**.

Process questions Based on work by Mehan (1979), these questions ask students to give opinions, interpretations and explanations.

Regional variation Differences in language forms that are linked to particular places.

Register Immediate context of situation described in terms of three aspects – the kind of activity or subject matter communicated in the **text**, the relationship between the writer and the reader or the speaker and the hearer, and the mode or channel of communication through which the text is produced.

Resolution The solving of a **problem** that occurred in the plot of a story.

Scaffolding The assistance and support offered by an expert to a novice to help the latter achieve a goal which would otherwise be difficult or impossible.

Second language acquisition Acquiring or learning a language after a first language has already been learned. Usually abbreviated as SLA. Sometimes distinguished from **second language learning** to contrast naturalistic acquisition as compared with intentional study or explicit instruction ('learning') such as in school settings. (This distinction is not highlighted in this volume.)

Second language instructional competence Refers to the stages of second language development in which learners are able to understand instruction and perform grade-level school activities using the second language alone in educational settings.

Second language learning Studying a language that is not the first language learned in life by the user, but within in a social context in which that language is commonly used (e.g. studying Portuguese in Brazil when the user's first language is German). Note that this is often used for studying a third, fourth, fifth (etc.) language. See also **second language acquisition**.

Semilingual The idea that some bilinguals might not have a full linguistic competence in either language. This idea has been strongly criticized as explained in Chapter 8.

Sequential bilingualism Those situations in which individuals become bilinguals later in their lives, frequently through school-based study.

Sharing time Discussed by Cazden (2001), this is an opportunity for students to share information based on their own experiences. It generally provides a chance for more extended student talk with the opportunity for the teacher to provide feedback or evaluation as a follow-up.

Simultaneous bilingualism Those situations in which children acquire two or more languages in their earliest childhood at the same time.

Skill transfer theory The theory proposes that the prior knowledge of learners influences positively the acquisition of new knowledge.

SLI (Specific language impairment) A developmental disorder characterized by delays and persistent weaknesses in language acquisition despite normal hearing, normal cognitive and socio-emotional development, and no frank neurological damage (e.g. no motor deficits, brain malformations or lesions).

Social dialectology Same as **variationist sociolinguistics**. This term emphasizes the fact that variationist sociolinguistics is a kind of **dialectology** that is particularly concerned with social variation.

Social variable In **Labovian sociolinguistics**, a way in which people in a particular community can be classified on the basis of their social characteristics, such as socio-economic status, gender, age and ethnicity.

Social variation Difference in form within a language that is linked to particular social groups in the same place (such as different social classes, genders, age-groups or ethnic groups).

Societal bilingualism Describes those countries, nations or communities that speak two or more languages.

Sociolinguistic interview The particular way of conducting an interview in **Labovian sociolinguistics**. In a sociolinguistic interview, a recording is made of an interview in which the social characteristics of the interviewee can be established, and evidence gained of their speech at the same time. A sociolinguistic interview includes specific activities that elicit different **styles**.

Sociolinguistic variable A **linguistic variable** that shows a particular pattern of use in a community, linked to **social variables**. A typical Labovian sociolinguistic variable is one in which the proportion of the more prestigious variant rises with the prestige of the speaker and with the level of formality of the **style**.

Sociolinguistics The study of how language works in a social context. Sociolinguistics is a major branch of **linguistics** and has many subdivisions. Its main concerns are with variation, bilingualism, language planning and expression of identity.

Solidarity A sense of unity or common purpose between or among people. This concept is used in **sociolinguistics** in discussion of forms that appeal to a sense of unity, friendliness or equality.

It is useful, for example, in understanding address terms and **accommodation**.

Speech acts Types of action or things performed or done through language.

Standard dialect The **dialect** given special prestige in a community. The standard dialect is the dialect of a language that is expected to be used in most writing and in formal circumstances. It is seen as the dialect suitable for education and the one to teach foreign learners. Standard dialects are often used over a wide geographical area, and for this reason some linguists would prefer the term 'standard variety'. The term 'standard language' is also sometimes used: The standard dialect is often seen as representing the whole language.

Status planning Language planning that addresses functional aspects of a language such as its role as a national language or **medium of instruction** in schools.

Structural ambiguity A sentence is ambiguous not because of any particular word(s), but because the words it contains can be grouped/structured in different ways, resulting in different interpretations.

Style Used in a number of different ways in linguistics. It is most usually defined as a way of using a language depending on the function of use or text type. In **Labovian sociolinguistics**, 'style' is a level of formality of speech reflecting how much attention is being paid to the speech. It is assumed that a speaker will use their more prestigious variants while paying the greatest attention to how they speak (such as when reading a list of words) and their least prestigious alternatives while paying the least attention (such as if they are emotionally engaged).

Stylization Term used in **identity sociolinguistics**, developed by Nikolas Coupland. The purposeful (and often playful) use of particular **linguistic forms** drawn from a **variety** not expected in the context, and different from the majority of forms in the same person's speech. See also **emblematic**, **indexical**, **criterial**.

Subtractive bilingualism The loss of one language in order to learn another language.

Synonyms Words which have the same or nearly the same meaning.

Syntax The study of how words can be put together to form phrases, and how phrases can be put together to form sentences.

Telegraphic speech A stage in language development when children use content words but often omit function words and bound **morphemes**.

Text The largest unit of linguistic structure which is above the level of clause and sentence.

Transfer (Also called 'cross-linguistic influence') A bilingual speaker's use of structures from one language (typically the L1) in the other language (typically the L2).

Translanguaging The usage of multiple languages according to the perspectives of bilinguals. See García (2009).

Underextension A child's use of a word with a meaning that is too narrow (e.g. *dog* = only the family's pet poodle). See **overextension**.

Utterance A term to refer to a short expression in spoken language (very roughly the spoken equivalent of a written sentence).

Variationist sociolinguistics The branch of **linguistics** founded by William Labov, which studies variation within a community using a particular methodology. Variationist sociolinguistics is concerned with looking at patterns of **social variation** within a single language in a particular community, and with considering how these patterns relate to the way in which languages change over time.

Variety A way of using a language that differs in form from some other way. This is an open term that can be used to refer to different **styles**, **dialects** or **accents**.

References

Accents and Dialects. London: British Library Board. Available at http://sounds.
bl.uk/Accents-and-dialects/

Alexander, R. J. (2008), *Towards Dialogic Teaching: Rethinking Classroom Talk*
(4th edn). Thirsk, North Yorkshire: Dialogos.

Andrews, S. (2007), *Language Teacher Awareness*. Cambridge: Cambridge
University Press.

Arias, M. B. and Faltis, C. (eds) (2012), *Implementing Educational Language
Policy in Arizona: Legal, Historical and Current Practices in SEI*. Bristol:
Multilingual Matters.

Baker, C. (2011), *Foundations of Bilingual Education and Bilingualism* (5th edn).
Clevedon, Avon: Multilingual Matters.

Ball, S. J. (2006), *Education Policy and Social Class: The Selected Works of
Stephen J. Ball*. London: Routledge.

Barnes, D. (1992), *From Communication to Curriculum* (2nd edn). Portsmouth,
NH: Boynton/Cook Publishers-Heinemann.

Berg, C., Hult, F. M. and King, K. A. (2001), 'Shaping the climate for language
shift? English in Sweden's elite domains'. *World Englishes*, 20 (3), 305–19.

Berger, J. (1972), *Ways of Seeing*. London: British Broadcasting Corporation and
Penguin Books.

Bialystok, E. (1987), 'Words as things: Development of word concept by
bilingual children'. *Studies in Second Language Acquisition*, 9.

—. (2011), 'Reshaping the mind: The benefits of bilingualism'. *Canadian Journal
of Experimental Psychology*, 65 (4), 229–35.

Bloomfield, L. (1933), *Language*. New York, NY: H. Holt and Company.

Borkin, A. and Reinhart, S. (1978), 'Excuse me and I'm sorry'. *TESOL Quarterly*,
12 (1), 57–69.

Brown, R. (1973), *A First Language: The Early Stages*. Cambridge, MA: Harvard
University Press.

Bull, T. (2012), 'Against the mainstream: Universities with an alternative
language policy'. *International Journal of the Sociology of Language*, 216,
55–73.

Cabau-Lampa, B. (2007), 'Mother tongue plus two European languages in
Sweden: Unrealistic educational goal?' *Language Policy*, 6, 333–58.

Carter, R., Goddard, A., Reah, D., Sanger, K. and Swift, N. (2008), *Working with
Texts: A Core Introduction to Language Analysis* (3rd edn). London and New
York, NY: Routledge.

Cazden, C. (2001), *Classroom Discourse: The Language of Teaching and
Learning* (2nd edn). Portsmouth, NH: Heinemann.

Christie, F. (2002), 'The development of abstraction in adolescence in subject
English'. In M. J. Schleppegrell and M. C. Colombi (eds), *Developing*

Advanced Literacy in First and Second Languages. Mahwah, NJ: Lawrence Erlbaum, pp. 45–66.

Compton, S. (2010), Implementing Language Policy for Deaf Students from Spanish-Speaking Homes: The Case of Agents in a Texas School District. Master's thesis, University of Texas at San Antonio. Available at http://gradworks.umi.com/14/75/1475894.html

Cooper, R. L. (1989), *Language Planning and Social Change*. New York, NY: Cambridge University Press.

Corbett, P. and Strong, J. (2011), *Talk for Writing across the Curriculum: How to Teach Non-Fiction Writing 5–12 Years*. Maidenhead: McGraw Hill Open University Press.

Coupland, N. (2007), *Style: Language Variation and Identity*. Cambridge: Cambridge University Press.

Craik, F. I. M., Bialystok, E. and Freeman, M. (2010), 'Delaying the onset of Alzheimer disease: Bilingualism as a form of cognitive reserve'. *Neurology*, 75, 1717–25.

Creese, A. and Blackledge, A. (2010), 'Translanguaging in the bilingual classroom: A pedagogy for learning and teaching?' *The Modern Language Journal*, 94 (i), 103–15.

Crystal, D. (2001/2006), *Language and the Internet*. Cambridge: Cambridge University Press.

Cummins, J. (1978), 'Metalinguistic development of children in bilingual education programs: Data from Irish and Canadian Ukranian-English programs'. In M. Paradis (ed.), *Aspects of Bilingualism*. Columbia, SC: Hornbeam Press.

—. (1979), 'Linguistic interdependence and the educational development of bilingual children'. *Review of Educational Research*, 49, 222–51.

Dewaele, J.-M. (2000), 'Three years old and three first languages'. *Bilingual Family Newsletter*, 17 (2), 4–5.

—. (2007), 'Becoming bi-or multi-lingual later in life'. In P. Auer and L. Wei (eds), *Handbook of Multilingualism and Multilingual Communication*. Berlin: Mouton de Gruyter, pp. 101–30.

Dickinson, D. K. and Tabors, P. O. (eds) (2001), *Beginning Literacy with Language*. Baltimore, MD: Paul H. Brookes.

Eckert, P. (2008), 'Variation and the indexical field'. *Journal of Sociolinguistics*, 12 (4), 453–76.

Edwards, J. (2008), 'The ecology of language: Insight and illusion'. In A. Creese, P. Martin and N. H. Hornberger (eds), *Encyclopedia of Language and Education, Volume 9: Ecology of Language*. New York, NY: Springer, pp. 15–26.

Fairclough, N. (1989), *Language and Power*. London: Longman.

Fenson, L., Marchman, V. A., Thal, D., Dale, P. S., Reznick, J. S. and Bates, E. (2006), *MacArthur-Bates Communicative Development Inventories: User's Guide and Technical Manual* (2nd edn). Baltimore, MD: Paul H. Brookes.

Ferguson, C. A. (1959), 'Diglossia'. *Word*, 15, 325–40.

Fisher, R., Myhill, D., Jones, S. and Larkin, S. (2010), *Using Talk to Support Writing*. London: Sage.

Fishman, J. A. (1980), 'Bilingualism and biculturism as individual and as societal phenomena'. *Journal of Multilingual and Multicultural Development*, 1, 3–15.

REFERENCES **189**

—. (2006), *Do Not Leave Your Language Alone: The Hidden Status Agendas within Corpus Planning in Language Policy*. Mahwah, NJ: Lawrence Erlbaum.

Fowler, R. (1991), *Language in the News: Discourse and Ideology in the Press*. London: Routledge.

García, O. (2009), *Bilingual Education in the 21st Century: A Global Perspective*. Malden, MA: Wiley-Blackwell.

Genesee, F. (2003), 'Rethinking bilingual acquisition'. In J. M. Dewaele (ed.), *Bilingualism: Challenges and Directions for Future Research*. Clevedon, Avon: Multilingual Matters, pp. 204–29.

—. (2004), 'What do we know about bilingual education for majority language students?' In T. K. Bhatia and W. Ritchie (eds), *Handbook of Bilingualism and Multiculturalism*. Malden, MA: Blackwell, pp. 547–76.

Giles, H. (1973), 'Accent mobility: A model and some data'. *Anthropological Linguistics*, 15 (2), 87–105.

Goh, C. C. M. and Burns, A. (2012), *Teaching Speaking: A Holistic Approach*. New York, NY: Cambridge University Press.

Goh, C. C. M. and Silver, R. E. (2006), *Language Learning: Home, School and Society*. Singapore: Longman, Pearson Education.

Grice, P. (1975), 'Logic and conversation'. In P. Cole and J. Morgan (eds), *Syntax and Semantics, Vol. 3: Speech Acts*. New York, NY: Academic Press, pp. 41–58.

Grosjean, F. (1982), *Life with Two Languages*. Cambridge, MA: Harvard University Press.

—. (1985), 'The bilingual as a competent but specific speaker-hearer'. *Journal of Multilingual and Multicultural Development*, 6, 467–77.

—. (2010), *Bilingual: Life and Reality*. Cambridge, MA: Harvard University Press.

Gupta, A. F. (2005), 'Baths and becks'. *English Today*, 81, 21–7.

Halliday, M. A. K. (1989), *Spoken and Written Language*. Oxford: Oxford University Press.

Halliday, M. A. K. and Hasan, R. (1976), *Cohesion in English*. London: Longman.

Hart, B. and Risley, T. (1995), *Meaningful Differences in the Everyday Experience of Young American Children*. Baltimore, MD: Paul H. Brookes.

Haugen, E. (1972), 'The ecology of language'. In A. Dil (ed.), *The Ecology of Language: Essays by Einar Haugen*. Stanford, CA: Stanford University Press, pp. 325–39.

Hockett, C. (1960), 'The origin of speech'. *Scientific American*, 203 (3), 88–96. Available at www.columbia.edu/~rmk7/HC/HC_Readings/Hockett.pdf

Hornberger, N. H. (2002), 'Multilingual language policies and the continua of biliteracy: An ecological approach'. *Language Policy*, 1, 27–51.

Hornberger, N. H. and Hult, F. M. (2008), 'Ecological language education policy'. In B. Spolsky and F. M. Hult (eds), *Handbook of Educational Linguistics*. Malden, MA: Blackwell, pp. 280–96.

Hult, F. M. (2010a), 'Analysis of language policy discourses across the scales of space and time'. *International Journal of the Sociology of Language*, 202, 7–24.

—. (2010b), 'Theme-based research in the transdisciplinary field of educational linguistics'. In F. M. Hult (ed.), *Directions and Prospects for Educational Linguistics*. New York, NY: Springer, pp. 19–32.

—. (2012), 'English as a transcultural language in Swedish policy and practice'. *TESOL Quarterly*, 46, 230–57.

Hult, F. M. and Compton, S. E. (2012), 'Deaf education policy as language policy: A comparative analysis of Sweden and the United States'. *Sign Language Studies*, 12, 602–20.

Jay, T. (2007), 'When young children use profanity: How to handle cursing and name calling'. *EarlychildhoodNEWS*. Excelligence Learning Corporation. Available at www.earlychildhoodnews.com/earlychildhood/article_print. aspx?ArticleId=59

Johnson, D. C. (2011), 'Implementational and ideological spaces in bilingual education policy, practice, and research'. In F. M. Hult and K. A. King (eds), *Educational Linguistics in Practice: Applying the Local Globally and the Global Locally*. Bristol: Multilingual Matters, pp. 126–39.

Kantor, K. J. and Rubin, D. L. (1981), 'Between speaking and writing: Processes of differentiation'. In B. M. Kroll and R. J. Vann (eds), *Exploring Speaking –Writing Relationships: Connections and Contrasts*. Urbana, IL: National Council of Teachers of English, pp. 55–81.

Kuhl, P. K. (2004), 'Early language acquisition: Cracking the speech code'. *Nature Reviews Neuroscience*, 5, 831–43.

Kuhl, P. K., Tsao, F.-M. and Liu, H.-M. (2003), 'Foreign-language experience in infancy: Effects of short-term exposure and social interaction on phonetic learning'. *Proceedings of the National Academy of Sciences*, 100, 9096–101.

Labov, W. (1966 repr. 1982), *The Social Stratification of English in New York City*. Washington, DC: Center for Applied Linguistics.

—. (2012), *William Labov: Home Page*. Available at www.ling.upenn. edu/~wlabov/

Ladefoged, P. (2006), *Vowels and Consonants* (5th edn). Boston, MA: Thomson/ Wadsworth Publishers.

Lambert, W. E. (1987), 'The effects of bilingual and bicultural experiences on children's attitudes and social perspectives'. In P. Homel, M. Palij and D. Aaronson (eds), *Childhood Bilingualism: Aspects of Linguistic Cognitive and Social Development*. Hillsdale, NJ: Lawrence Erlbaum, pp. 197–221.

Lanza, E. (2007), 'Multilingualism and the family'. In P. Auer and L. Wei (eds), *Handbook of Multilingualism and Multilingual Communication*. Berlin: Mouton de Gruyter, pp. 45–67.

Le Page, R. B. and Tabouret-Keller, A. (1985), *Acts of Identity: Creole-Based Approaches to Language and Ethnicity*. Cambridge: Cambridge University Press.

Lee-Wong, S. M. (1994), 'Imperatives in requests: Direct or impolite – observations from Chinese'. *Pragmatics*, 4, 491–515.

Lenneberg, E. (1967), *Biological Foundations of Language*. New York, NY: Wiley.

Levelt, W. J. M. (1989), *Speaking: From Intention to Articulation*. Cambridge, MA: The MIT Press.

Lwin, S. M. and Teo, P. (2011), 'Examining transitional cues in oral storytelling discourse to help students in narrative writing'. Paper presented at the 3rd New Zealand Discourse Conference, Engaging with Discourse Analysis, 5–7 December 2011, AUT University, Auckland, New Zealand.

Mehan, H. (1979), *Learning Lessons: Social Organization in the Classroom.* Cambridge, MA: Harvard University Press.

Menken, K. (2008), *English Language Learners Left Behind: Standardized Testing as Language Policy.* Bristol: Multilingual Matters.

Menken, K. and García, O. (eds) (2010), *Negotiating Language Policies in Schools: Educators as Policymakers.* London: Routledge.

Mercer, N. (1995), *The Guided Construction of Knowledge: Talk Amongst Teachers and Learners.* Clevedon, Avon: Multilingual Matters.

—. (1996), 'The quality of talk in children's collaborative activity in the classroom'. *Learning and Instruction,* 6, 359–77.

—. (2000), *Words & Minds: How We Use Language to Think Together.* New York, NY: Routledge.

—. (2002), 'Developing dialogues'. In G. Wells and G. Claxton (eds), *Learning for Life in the 21st Century: Sociocultural Perspectives on the Future of Education.* Oxford, UK: Blackwell, pp. 141–53.

—. (2007), 'English as a classroom language'. In N. Mercer, J. Swann and B. Mayor (eds), *Learning English.* Abingdon, UK: Routledge, pp. 117–49.

Mercer, N., Warwick, P., Kershner, R. and Staarman, J. K. (2010), 'Can the interactive whiteboard help to provide "dialogic space" for children's collaborative activity?' *Language and Education,* 24, 367–84.

Minami, M. (2008), 'Telling good stories in different languages: Bilingual children's styles of story construction and their linguistic and educational implication'. *Narrative Inquiry,* 18 (1), 83–110.

Moje, E. B. (2008), 'Foregrounding the disciplines in secondary literacy teaching and learning: A call for change'. *Journal of Adolescent & Adult Literacy,* 52 (2), 96–107.

Moje, E., Overby, M., Tysvaer, N. and Morris, K. (2008), 'The complex world of adolescent literacy: Myths, motivations, and mysteries'. *Harvard Educational Review,* 78 (1), 107–54.

Moore, C., Angelopoulos, M. and Bennett, P. (1999), 'Word learning in the context of referential and salience cues'. *Developmental Psychology,* 35, 60–8.

Ogiermann, E. (2009), 'Politeness and in-directness across cultures: A comparison of English, German, Polish and Russian requests'. *Journal of Politeness Research,* 5 (2), 189–216.

Orton, H., Sanderson, S. and Widdowson, J. (1978), *The Linguistic Atlas of England.* London: Croom Helm.

Paradis, J. (2007), 'Early bilingual and multilingual acquisition'. In P. Auer and L. Wei (eds), *Handbook of Multilingualism and Multilingual Communication.* Berlin: Mouton de Gruyter, pp. 15–44.

Pearson, B. Z., Fernández, S. C., Lewedeg, V. and Oller, D. K. (1997), 'The relation of input factors to lexical learning by bilingual infants'. *Applied Psycholinguistics,* 18, 41–58.

Reagan, T. G. (2010), *Language Policy and Planning for Sign Languages.* Washington, DC: Gallaudet University Press.

Resnick, L. B., Michaels, S. and O'Connor, M. C. (2010), 'How (well-structured) talk builds the mind'. In D. D. Preiss and R. L. Sternberg (eds), *Innovations in Educational Psychology: Perspectives on Learning, Teaching and Human Development.* New York, NY: Springer, pp. 163–94.

Rolstad, K. and MacSwan, J. (2008), 'BICS/CALP: Theory and critique'. In
    J. Gonzalez (ed.), *Encyclopedia of Bilingual Education*. Thousand Oaks, CA:
    Sage, pp. 62–5.
Rubin, D. L. and Kang, O. (2008), 'Writing to speak: What goes on across
    the two-way street'. In Belcher, D. and Hirvela, A. (eds), *The Oral-Literate
    Connection: Perspectives on L2 Speaking, Writing and Other Media
    Instructions*. Ann Arbor, MI: University of Michigan Press, pp. 210–25.
Ruíz, R. (1984), 'Orientations in language planning'. *NABE Journal*, 8 (2), 15–34.
Saffran, J. R., Aslin, R. N. and Newport, E. L. (1996), 'Statistical learning by
    eight-month-old infants'. *Science*, 274, 1926–8.
Sankoff, G. and LaBerge, S. (1973), 'On the acquisition of native speakers by a
    language'. *Kivung*, 6, 32–47.
Schiffman, H. F. (1996), *Linguistic Culture and Language Policy*. London and
    New York, NY: Routledge.
Searle, J. R. (1992), *The Rediscovery of the Mind*. Cambridge, MA: The MIT
    Press.
Secada, W. G. and Carey, D. A. (1990, October), 'Teaching mathematics with
    understanding to limited English proficient students'. Urban Diversity Series
    No.101. ERIC Clearinghouse on Urban Education Institute on Urban and
    Minority Education (ERIC Document Reproduction Service No. ED322284).
Shanahan, T. and Shanahan, C. (2008), 'Teaching disciplinary literacy to
    adolescents: Rethinking content area literacy'. *Harvard Educational Review*,
    78 (1), 40–59.
Shohamy, E. (2006), *Language Policy: Hidden Agendas and New Approaches*.
    New York, NY: Routledge.
Singleton, J. L. and Newport, E. L. (2004), 'When learners surpass their
    models: The acquisition of American Sign Language from inconsistent input'.
    Cognitive Psychology, 49, 370–407.
Skutnabb-Kangas, T. (2000), *Linguistic Genocide in Education – Or Worldwide
    Diversity and Human Rights?* Mahwah, NJ: Lawrence Erlbaum.
Snow, S. E., Tabors, P. O., Nicholson, P. A. and Kurland, B. F. (1995), 'SHELL:
    Oral language and early literacy skills in kindergarten and first-grade children'.
    Journal of Research on Childhood Education, 10, 37–48.
Spolsky, B. (2004), *Language Policy*. New York, NY: Cambridge University
    Press.
Swales, J. M. (1990), *Genre Analysis: English in Academic and Research
    Settings*. Cambridge: Cambridge University Press.
Van der Walt, C., Mabule, D. R. and De Beer J. J. (2001), 'Letting the L1 in by
    the back door: Codeswitching and translation in science, mathematics, and
    biology classes'. *SAALT Journal*, 35 (2 and 3), 170–84.
Walter, S. L. (2008), 'The language of instruction issue: Framing an empirical
    perspective'. In B. Spolsky and F. M. Hult (eds), *The Handbook of Educational
    Linguistics*. Malden, MA: Blackwell, pp. 129–46.
Weissberg, R. (2006), *Connecting Speaking & Writing in Second Language
    Writing Instruction*. Ann Arbor, MI: Michigan Series on Teaching Multilingual
    Writers.
Wells, G. (1992), 'The centrality of talk in education'. In K. Norman (ed.),
    Thinking Voices: The Works of the National Oracy Project. London: Hodder &
    Stoughton.

Werker, J. T. and Tees, R. C. (1984), 'Cross-language speech perception: Evidence from perceptual reorganization during the first year of life'. *Infant Behavior and Development*, 7, 49–63.

Whitney, D. M. J. (2012), A Discourse Analysis of U.S. National and State Language Policies: Restraining English Instruction for Refugee Adults. Master's thesis, University of Texas at San Antonio. Available at http://gradworks.umi.com/15/18/1518712.html

Widdowson, H. G. (2007), *Discourse Analysis*. Oxford: Oxford University Press.

Wiley T. G. (1996), 'Language planning and policy'. In S. L. McKay and N. H. Hornberger (eds), *Sociolinguistics and Language Teaching*. New York, NY: Cambridge University Press, pp. 103–47.

Woodson, K. (2010), Discursive Relationships between Dominant US Language Policy Ideologies and the Congressional Record in Relation to Title III of the No Child Left Behind Act of 2001. Master's thesis, University of Texas at San Antonio.

Yule, G. (2010), *The Study of Language* (4th edn). Cambridge: Cambridge University Press.

Index